# TABLE OF CONTENTS

## Astonishing Animals and Plants

| | |
|---|---|
| What a Star! | 4 |
| Plentiful Panda Poo | 8 |
| Best Friends Forever | 12 |
| Purple Frogs!? | 16 |
| Dragon's Blood | 20 |
| Elvis Impersonator | 24 |
| Tree-Climbing Goats | 28 |
| Plant Architecture | 32 |
| Brainy Birds | 36 |
| A Helping Hand | 40 |
| Lizards Fight Back | 44 |
| No Sweet Tooth Here | 48 |
| The Look-Alikes | 52 |
| Dead or Alive? | 56 |

## Curious Customs

| | |
|---|---|
| Bathroom Buddies | 60 |
| Beware of Alligator | 64 |
| A Birthday Bite | 68 |
| Barf Bags | 72 |
| Smash Bash | 76 |
| Food Fight | 80 |
| Celebrate This! | 84 |
| Trick or Turkey | 88 |
| Dress in Style | 92 |
| Medical Remedies | 96 |
| Beauty Secrets | 100 |
| Help Wanted | 104 |

## Awesome Anatomy

| | |
|---|---|
| Mirror, Mirror | 108 |
| Hair Where!? | 112 |
| Watch What I Can Do! | 116 |
| Foot Families | 120 |
| Walking in Circles | 124 |
| A Rush of Blush | 128 |

## Odd Objects

| | |
|---|---|
| VW Sausages | 132 |
| Up Periscope! | 136 |
| Make Your Mark | 140 |
| An Apple a Day | 144 |
| Thank the Military | 148 |
| Don't Bug Me! | 152 |
| What's for Dinner? | 156 |
| Say What? | 160 |
| A Better Mousetrap | 164 |
| Bitty Bots | 168 |
| Food Fads | 172 |
| A Cleaner History | 176 |

## Peculiar Places

| | |
|---|---|
| Squirrel Crossing | 180 |
| Underwater Hotel | 184 |
| Monkey Island | 188 |
| Origami on the Move | 192 |
| Rainbow Mountains | 196 |
| It's Raining What!? | 200 |
| Space Stinks! | 204 |
| Blue Fire | 208 |
| The Loneliest Place | 212 |

| | |
|---|---|
| **Answer Key** | 216 |

# UNUSUALLY FUN

GRADE 5

# FUN

## READING & MATH

### SERIOUSLY FUN TOPICS TO TEACH SERIOUSLY IMPORTANT SKILLS

Carson Dellosa Education
Greensboro, North Carolina

The facts presented in this book are for informational and entertainment purposes only. The nature of extreme facts makes them difficult to authenticate. Carson Dellosa Education makes no warranty as to the reliability, accuracy, timeliness, usefulness, or completeness of the facts contained herein.

**Credits**
Authors: Chris Schwab, Jennifer Stith, Hailey Scragg
Cover Design: Joshua Janes
Interior Design: Joshua Janes, Lynne Schwaner, Max Porter

Carson Dellosa Education
PO Box 35665
Greensboro, NC 27425
carsondellosa.com

© 2023, Carson Dellosa Education. The purchase of this material entitles the buyer to reproduce worksheets and activities for classroom use only—not for commercial resale. Reproduction of these materials for an entire school or district is prohibited. No part of this book may be reproduced (except as noted above), stored in a retrieval system, or transmitted in any form or by any means (mechanically, electronically, recording, etc.) without the prior written consent of Carson Dellosa Education.

Printed in the USA • All rights reserved.
02-078247784

ISBN 978-1-4838-6714-4

# WHAT A STAR!

The star-nosed mole has a peculiar nose. It is surrounded by 22 tiny armlike tentacles. This mole may be the weirdest-looking animal on Earth, but, its nose is its superpower.

Star-nosed moles use their noses for everything, but mostly to find food. Their favorite foods are worms and bugs. They eat faster than any other animal. These critters can find and eat a bug in less than two-tenths of a second!

You may never see a star-nosed mole, but if you're ever in the wet, marshy areas of the eastern United States and Canada, be on the lookout! Look for a small animal, about eight inches (20 cm) long. Short, dark fur hides its tiny ears. It can barely see with its beady eyes, so this mole finds its way around with its nose. The mole's tail is scaly and a little hairy. Its feet are large and tipped with long, pointy claws for digging tunnels. But, you'll know it instantly by its awesome nose.

STAR-NOSED MOLE

This mole's incredible nose helps it find food, even under water. It may be the only animal that can smell under water. The mole blows a bubble into the water, then takes it back in to sniff for prey.

**Write a response to each question.**

1. What is the main idea of the passage?

_____

_____

2. Identify a key detail that supports the main idea.

_____

_____

**Match each word to its definition.**

3. tentacle                covered with scales

4. marshy                  wet and muddy with thick grasses

5. scaly                   a long, thin armlike part, usually on a head or mouth

I'M A "MOLEY" STAR!

**Answer each question.**

1. A star-nosed mole has approximately 25,000 sense receptors on its nose. Which is NOT an expression for 25,000?

   250 × 100       1,000 × 25       2 × 5,000       10 × 2,500

2. A star-nosed mole has approximately 22 armlike tentacles on its nose. If there are 100 star-nosed moles, which expression describes how many tentacles there are in all?

   0.10 × 2200       1 × 220       100 × 22       0.01 × 2200

**Solve each problem.**

3. Six star-nosed moles eat 20 worms each for 7 days. How many worms did they eat in all?

   _____ worms

4. Ten star-nosed moles eat 18 worms each day for 5 days. How many worms did they eat in all?

   _____ worms

**Follow the directions.**

Help the star-nosed mole find food. Draw a line through the path of bubbles that have fractions in simplest form.

START

| | | |
|---|---|---|
| 1/2 | 2/4 | 3/6 |
| 2/5 | 1/5 | 5/10 | 4/6 |
| 1/4 | 6/8 | 8/10 | 4/8 |
| 2/3 | 3/4 | 3/5 | 6/12 |
| 8/12 | 2/10 | 1/2 | |

FINISH

# PLENTIFUL PANDA POO

Giant pandas are black and white and cute all over. They also poop all over. In fact, pandas poop up to 40 times a day. That's a lot of panda poo!

*SMELLS LIKE LEAVES WITH A HINT OF ROOTS.*

Pandas eat a simple, almost completely vegetarian diet. Adult pandas chow down on about 30 pounds (14 kg) of bamboo every day. They mostly eat its roots, shoots, stems, and leaves. But, pandas find bamboo difficult to digest. Their gut bacteria only work on 17 percent of all that bamboo. So, what happens to the rest of it?

You guessed it. Pandas poop it out. You can tell which part of the bamboo plant they were eating by the color of the droppings. Green poo means they were eating leaves, while yellow poo indicates stems. Because pandas poop so much, the average plop measures only 6 inches (15 cm) long.

PANDA'S POOP

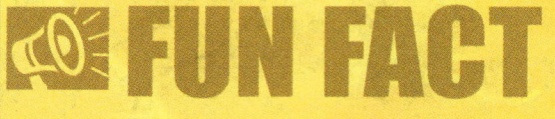

In case you were wondering, pandas pee while hanging upside down on a tree trunk. They climb the tree in a handstand position so they can leave their mark higher up. What an animal!

**Answer each question.**

1. *Plentiful Panda Poo* is an example of which type of figurative language?

    A. personification

    B. alliteration

    C. hyperbole

2. The word *vegetarian* means

    A. one who eats only fish and meat.

    B. one who eats from a garden.

    C. one who eats only vegetables, fruits, nuts, and grains.

3. How much of a panda's food is digested in its gut?

    A. 17 percent

    B. 100 percent

    C. 15 percent

**Write an antonym for each word from the text.**

simple _____

difficult _____

**Solve each problem.**

1. At the zoo, the Giant Panda Cam lets viewers watch live while Ling-Ling and Hsing-Hsing eat bamboo. Ling-Ling eats 32 pounds of food each day. Hsing-Hsing eats 16 pounds of food each day. How much would each panda eat by the end of one week?

   Ling-Ling eats _____ pounds.     Hsing-Hsing eats _____ pounds.

2. Zhen-Zhen the giant panda eats 160 pounds of bamboo at the end of 5 days. Xi-Lan the giant panda eats 115 pounds at the end of 5 days. How much did each panda eat per day on average?

   Zhen-Zhen eats _____ pounds.     Xi-Lan eats _____ pounds.

3. Explain a similarity between Ling-Ling and Zhen-Zhen.

   _____

   _____

   _____

   _____

   _____

I'M ON THE PANDA CAM!

**Follow the directions.**

Color the boxes that contain prime numbers to help Tuan-Tuan find the bamboo.

| 2 | 3 | 1 | 4 |
|---|---|---|---|
| 6 | 5 | 7 | 11 |
| 10 | 8 | 12 | 13 |
| 29 | 23 | 19 | 17 |
| 31 | 32 | 39 | 24 |
| 37 | 41 | 44 | 50 |
| 45 | 43 | 47 | 51 |
| 58 | 57 | 53 | 56 |

# BEST FRIENDS FOREVER

The pearlfish and the sea cucumber have an odd relationship. It's hard to explain. First, you need to know more about them.

The pearlfish is a long, skinny fish with a body like an eel. It is mostly transparent. You can almost see through it. Pearlfish live primarily in the shallow waters of the Pacific, Atlantic, and Indian Oceans.

Sea cucumbers live there too. The sea cucumber is a funny looking creature that resembles a pickle! Its dark body is long and tube-shaped. Because it is an invertebrate, the sea cucumber has no backbone. And can you believe this? A sea cucumber poops and breathes from the same hole. It breathes by allowing water into its butt!

So back to the hard-to-explain relationship between these two sea creatures: when the sea cucumber "breathes" a pearlfish may dart in its opening. The pearlfish fears larger fish and quickly needs shelter. The tiny intruder hangs out in the sea cucumber's intestines. It may pop out to get food but often nibbles away at the sea cucumber's guts. As many as 15 pearlfish have been seen wiggling out of a single sea cucumber's butt.

Pearlfish are freeloaders! They also live rent free inside pearl oysters, starfish, and other invertebrates.

**Match each word to its definition.**

1. transparent    one that enters without an invitation

2. invertebrate    easy to see through

3. intruder    the lower part of the digestive system

4. intestines    not having a backbone or spine

**Write a response to the question.**

5. How does the author describe the relationship between a pearlfish and a sea cucumber?

_____

_____

_____

**Solve each problem.**

1. A pearlfish is looking for shelter. It is 0.14 hundredths of a mile from the nearest sea cucumber. After swimming 0.3 tenths of the distance, it stops to eat. How much of a mile has it swum?

   _____ miles

2. The pearlfish finds shelter in a sea cucumber. The sea cucumber moves its location an additional 0.23 hundredths of a mile from the pearlfish's starting point. How far is the pearlfish from its original location?

   _____ feet

3. The pearlfish decides to move to a new shelter. An oyster is 0.24 miles away. A starfish is 0.12 miles away. Which invertebrate is closer? How much closer? Explain.

4. The _____ is closer by

   _____

   _____

   _____

**Follow the directions.**

Use addition, subtraction, multiplication, and/or division to form an expression with the given digits. The expression should equal the given number.

Ex. **Make 12**
 1  2  4  5
 (4 x 5) – (4 x 2)   **or**   2 x 4 + 5 – 1   **or**   14 - 2

**1.** Make 30

 6  2  9  5  3

**2.** Make 75

 2  9  1  7  2  5

**3.** Make 110

 1  2  4  5  7  8

# PURPLE FROGS!?

PIGNOSE FROG

The India Purple frog, or pignose frog, is quite peculiar looking. In a world of mostly brown and green frogs, this frog is purplish-gray. Its head is unusual too and looks more like the head of a mole. Its distinctive pig-like snout is pointy on the end. The pignose frog uses its unusual nose to slurp up ants and termites underground. Its legs are short, strong, and tipped with tough claws. And its body appears bloated and round.

Found in the Western Ghats of India, the pignose frog only comes above ground a few weeks a year during the rainy season. Its goal is to find a mate. The male is one third the length of a female. To attract a large, bloated beauty, the male calls out to her. The pignose frog doesn't sound like a frog, either. Instead of saying, "Ribbit," it sounds more like a clucking chicken. What an odd frog!

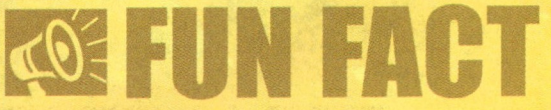 Local people in the Western Ghats of India often consume pignose frogs. They find the creature to be quite delicious.

**Write T for *true* or F for *false*.**

_____ 1. A pignose frog gets embarrassed easily.

_____ 2. It has a snout like a pig.

_____ 3. It spends most of its life underground.

_____ 4. It mostly eats ants and termites.

_____ 5. It sounds like other frogs.

**Answer the question.**

6. What does the author NOT think or say about the pignose frog?

   A. The author thinks it is quite unusual.

   B. The author calls it *odd*.

   C. The author thinks it has problems.

   D. The author describes it as *peculiar looking*.

I'M PECULIAR, PURPLE, AND PERFECT!

**Complete each table.**

1. A male pignose frog is $\frac{1}{3}$ the length of a female pignose frog. How long is each frog? Use the measurements in the table.

| Male | Female |
|---|---|
| 3 inches | |
| 2.7 inches | 8.1 inches |
| | 10.5 inches |
| 1.8 inches | |
| | 7.2 inches |

2. If a pignose frog makes 126 clucking sounds in one minute, then how many sounds could it make in the number of seconds in each column?

| Time in Seconds | 10 | 20 | 30 | 40 | 50 | 60 |
|---|---|---|---|---|---|---|
| Number of Clucks | | | | | | 126 |

**Solve each problem.**

3. 6.3 ÷ 9 = _____

5. 9.6 ÷ 8 = _____

4. 2.2 × 4 = _____

6. 4.5 × 3 = _____

**Follow the directions.**

Find and circle ten adjectives that the author used to describe the pignose frog. (Hint: Reread the text and make a list.)

```
A R O F P G L A R G E L D S K
F P P G L H Q G O M J I J O H
G O S H Y J W H U C N P G Y R
H I O H H K E D N X G U H R F
J U I N O L R S D Z B R J Q U
S T N M G R T E I P N P E T O
T O G U F O T S J E C L A E C
R Y F P S A Y A H C D E T M N
O U D H O U U Z G U G R O W O
N I S L Q I A X F L B F O D D
G K B F W U N L B I N R I D P
K I A C E Y N T V A B J O K L
L K Z X R T B V Y R P D Z X K
```

# DRAGON'S BLOOD

With a name like the Socotra dragon tree, or dragon's blood tree, you have to wonder how it got its name. If you cut this tree, it will bleed! It is not really blood, but it looks like it. The liquid is deep red, like the fire from a dragon. It has no taste or smell. What looks like blood is just red sap, or resin.

SOCOTRA DRAGON'S BLOOD TREE

DRAGON'S BLOOD RESIN

This particular tree grows on Socotra, a tiny island in the Indian Ocean off the coast of Yemen. It is one of the most unusual trees in the world. Branches spread out from the trunk like the spokes of an enormous umbrella. There are no leaves on the branches except at the very top. The leaves are spiky and point upward, like pineapple leaves. In March, white or green flowers grow in its "crown."

The blood-red sap has been used to treat medical problems such as wounds and burns. It was thought to improve human digestion and be good for human blood. Dragon's tree resin can stop bleeding anywhere inside the body. It helps it clot more easily to close wounds. The sap has also been used to make toothpaste, ink, lipstick, and varnish for violins. What a useful tree!

**FUN FACT** — The dragon's blood tree's wood is used in human-made beehives. The bees produce red honey. It is one of the most expensive honeys in the world.

**Write a response to each question.**

1. When you read the title, what did you think the passage would be about?

_____

_____

2. Write two things that surprised you in this passage.

_____

_____

**Match each part of the simile or metaphor from the text.**

3. tree                                        pineapple leaves

4. branches                                    crown

5. leaves                                      umbrella

6. treetop                                     spokes

LOOKS LIKE SOMEONE NEEDS A BANDAGE!

**Complete the factor tree for each number.**

**Example:**

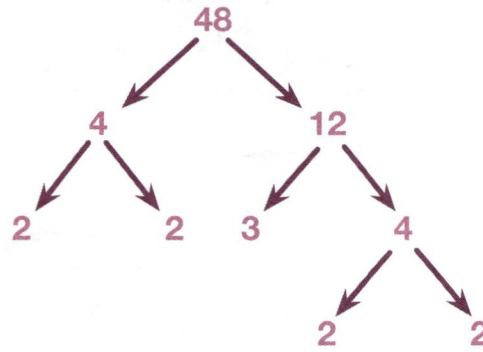

1.

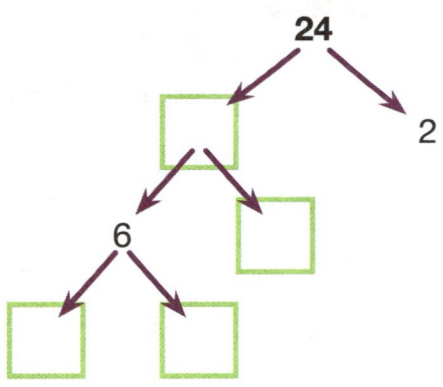

2.

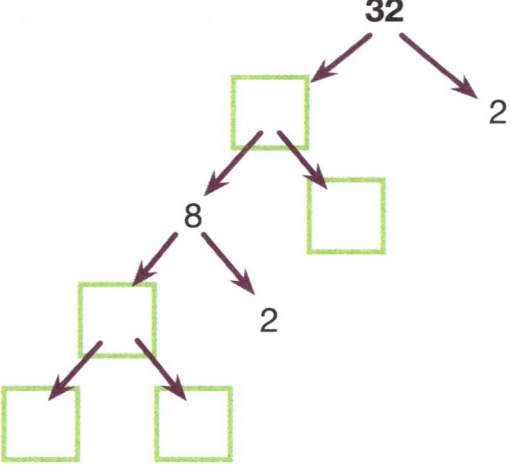

3.

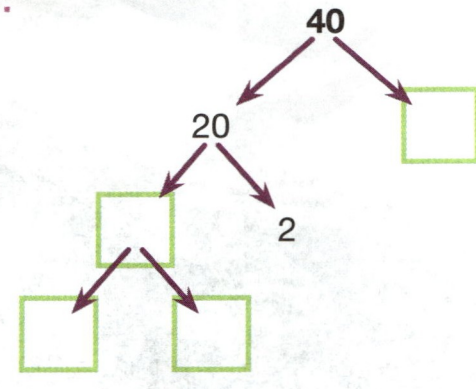

4.

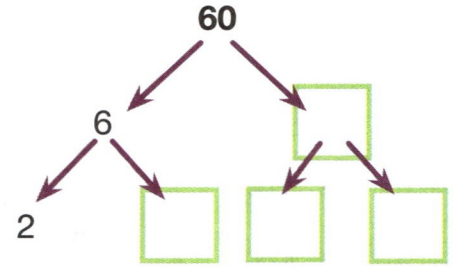

**Follow the directions.**

Try making new words from the letters in *Socotra Dragon*. Make different words of various lengths.

# S O C O T R A    D R A G O N

two-letter word: _____ _____

three-letter word: _____ _____ _____

four-letter word: _____ _____ _____ _____

five-letter word: _____ _____ _____ _____ _____

six-letter word: _____ _____ _____ _____ _____ _____

seven-letter word: _____ _____ _____ _____ _____ _____ _____

# ELVIS IMPERSONATOR

You may be too young to know about singer Elvis Presley, who was wildly popular and known as "The King of Rock and Roll." But, ask your grandparents about Elvis's hairstyle. Then, compare it to the crest on top of the long-wattled umbrellabird. Maybe they had the same stylist!

"THANK YOU. THANK YOU VERY MUCH."

LONG-WATTLED UMBRELLABIRD

The long-wattled umbrellabird lives in parts of South America. It could win prizes for Fanciest Bird. First, its bushy feather crest looks like it was combed forward. Like Elvis's hair, it hangs well past the bird's eyes and juts out over its bill. A long wattle dangles below the bill and is as long as 11 inches (28 cm). In a quiet moment, it looks like a dark necktie. But, when the bird is excited, it inflates. Then, the wattle's short, scaly feathers make it look like a pinecone!

During mating season, male umbrellabirds gather in one place. The females come to pick out the best mate. The male umbrellabirds show off to attract them. They raise their crests, inflate their wattles, and make loud sounds that can be heard a mile away, as if to say, "Pick me, pick me!"

Long-wattled umbrellabirds are lousy fliers. They prefer to spend their time in the middle of trees so they can hop from branch to branch. If an umbrellabird has to fly, it pulls in its wattle first.

**Write a response to each question.**

1. Write a different title for this passage. Make it fun!

_____

_____

2. Why did the author compare the umbrellabird to Elvis Presley?

_____

_____

3. List three things the umbrellabird does to attract a mate.

_____

_____

_____

4. The author used words to "paint" a picture in the reader's mind. Draw the bird in the box. Label it with the words.

**Round the numbers to solve each problem.**

1. A scientist is studying male umbrellabirds in their habitat. She counts approximately 58 male umbrellabirds in the area. If the umbrellabird's wattle is on average 11 inches long, about how many inches in total are all the male birds' wattles together?

   _____ inches

2. If another scientist approximates about 616 cm in length for all the male umbrellabirds in his area, about how many birds did he count? (An umbrellabird has on average a 28-cm-long wattle.)

   _____ umbrellabirds

**Write a response to the question.**

3. How does rounding numbers help you solve the problems?

   _____

   _____

   _____

   _____

ANYONE GOT A COMB?

# Follow the directions.

Divide to find each quotient. Match each quotient with the correct letter in the key. To solve the riddle, write the letters in order on the answer lines.

**Question**: Which animal never needs a haircut?

| 19 = E | 24 = B | 37 = G | 43 = A | 55 = L | 82 = D |

1. 22)946

2. 37)888

3. 21)903

4. 15)825

5. 99)8,118

6. 64)1,216

7. 61)2,623

8. 49)1,813

9. 34)1,870

10. 85)1,615

Answer: _____  _____ _____ _____ _____

_____ _____ _____ _____ _____

# TREE-CLIMBING GOATS

Yes! Goats are quite nimble and can climb trees, and they almost never fall. In Morocco, Africa, Tamri goats can be seen balancing in argan trees to eat the fruit and leaves. Argan trees are prickly and thorny, so many creatures avoid foraging in them. But, goats go to the extremes for the tasty fruit they can't get enough of.

Many argan trees were planted by climbing goats. What!? How do goats plant trees? Scientists believe these goats start new trees all the time by eating the fruit and then excreting or spitting out the seeds. Over time, the seed grows into another argan tree.

And what makes these goats great at balancing on the argan tree branches?

TAMRI GOATS FORAGING IN AN ARGAN TREE

It is not from hours of playing *The Floor is Lava*! Goats have cloven feet. Each hoof has two toes that can spread apart and the soles are soft to allow goats to grip the branches. The goats use their dewclaws to pull up on branches or lower themselves from the trees.

 **FUN FACT** Some people collect the argan seeds goats leave behind. The seeds are processed so argan oil can be extracted and sold. The valuable oil is used in hair, beauty, and food products.

**Answer each question.**

1. How is the text organized?

    A. compare and contrast

    B. sequence

    C. description

    D. cause and effect

2. According to the text, how do argan goats help people make money?

    A. Goat herders get paid to look after them.

    B. They plant more argan trees.

    C. People sell the argan seeds the goats leave behind.

    D. Argan goats prune the argan trees.

**Find a synonym in the text for each word or phrase.**

3. over the top _____

4. eliminating _____

5. pricey _____

# Complete the table and graph.

Ayad and Habib collect argan seeds from goats' droppings for 10 minutes. The table shows how much each person collected. Use the pattern to complete the table.

| Minutes | Ayad | Habib |
|---|---|---|
| 0 | 0 | 0 |
| 1 | 3 | 5 |
| 2 | 6 | 10 |
| 3 | | |
| 4 | | |
| 5 | | |
| 6 | | |
| 7 | | |
| 8 | | |
| 9 | | |
| 10 | | |

Use the data to make a line graph. Use a different color to represent each person.

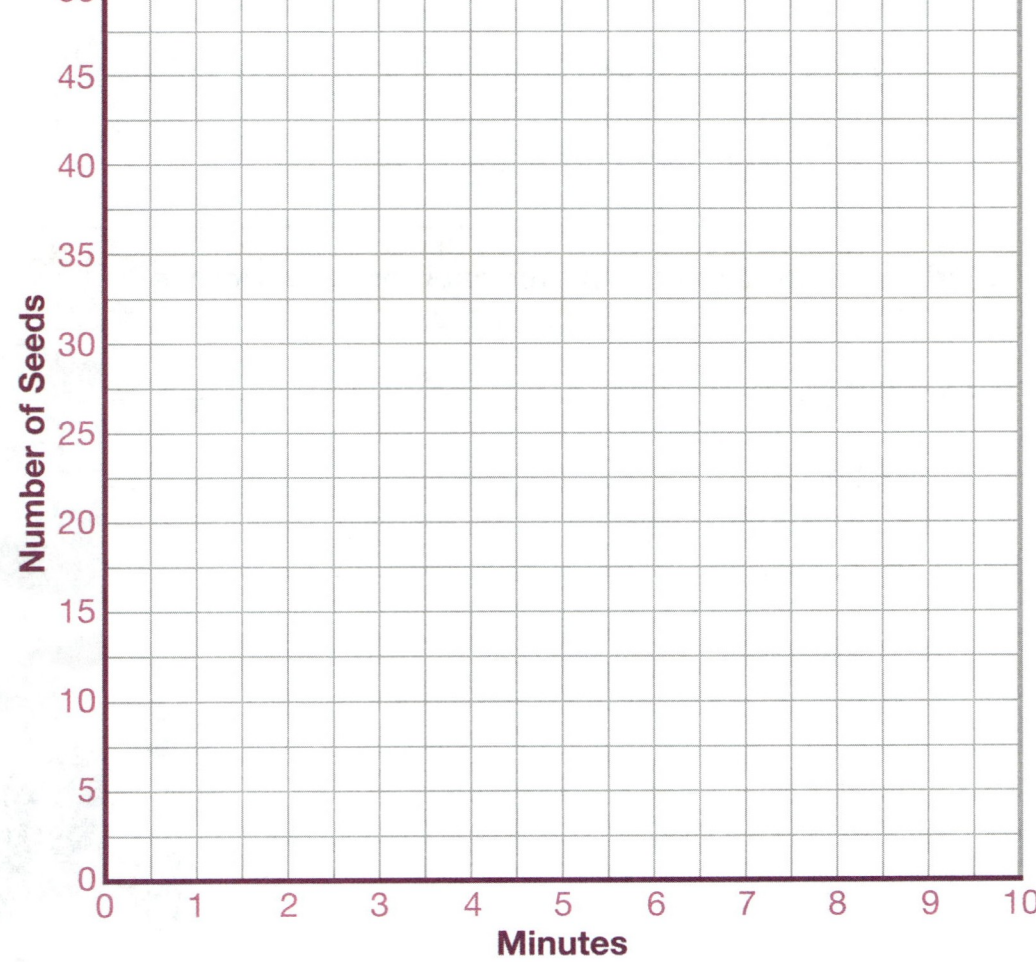

■ Ayad
■ Habib

**Follow the directions.**

Some goats excreted seeds on the ground. Use the coordinates to plot the locations of the seeds.

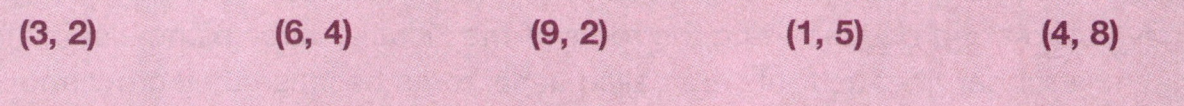

| (3, 2) | (6, 4) | (9, 2) | (1, 5) | (4, 8) |
| (5, 1) | (4, 6) | (9, 6) | (2, 9) | (7, 8) |

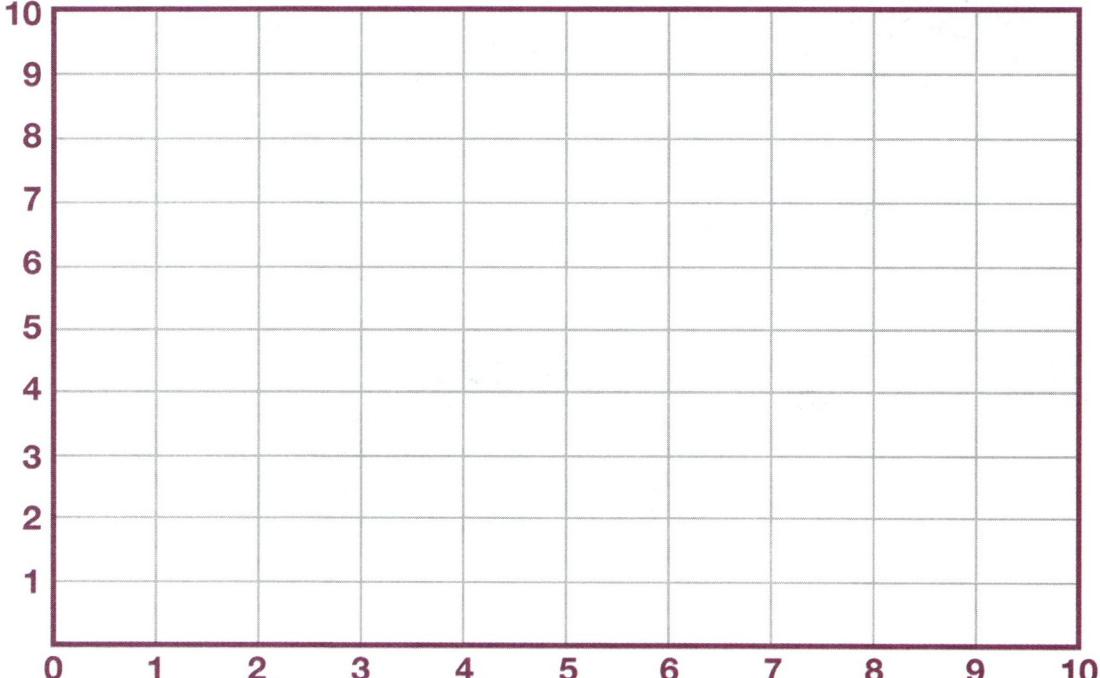

# PLANT ARCHITECTURE

Have you ever crossed a bridge that was alive? That grows and changes over time? For centuries, villagers have been walking across living bridges in places like Meghalaya, India. This village is quite remote, and supplies are hard to get. They build strong bridges using the roots of the *Ficus elastica* plant, also named the India rubber tree. Its roots are called aerial roots because they grow above the ground.

A BRIDGE FORMED FROM THE FICUS ELASTICA PLANT

Living bridges are built by first planting a *Ficus elastica* shoot on one side of a river or canyon. The villagers watch for the roots to start growing out from the plant. Then, they wind them onto a frame, usually made of bamboo, that stretches across the river. When the roots reach the other side, they are planted in the soil there. These roots produce more roots that reach into the air. Villagers watch and train them to bend and turn to strengthen the bridge.

As the living bridge grows, additional features may be added. These may include handrails and even a second deck to walk on. Wouldn't it be interesting to take a picture once a year and compare them?

**FUN FACT** — This plant also grows in Central America. The early Aztecs used the sap of this plant to make shoes and to waterproof their clothing.

**Complete each sentence with a word from the word bank.**

| aerial | frame | produce | remote |
|---|---|---|---|

1. The *Ficus elastica* puts out _____ roots.

2. Villagers who live in _____ villages build bridges using what they have.

3. Ficus roots are trained to grow around a _____ that crosses a river or canyon.

4. When those roots are planted on the other side, they _____ more roots.

**Write F for *fact* or O for *opinion*.**

_____ 5. It would be interesting to take a picture once a year and compare them.

_____ 6. They build strong bridges using the roots of the *Ficus elastica* plant.

THIS IS NOT IN THE "PLANTS"!

**Follow the directions.**

Draw a line to create a bridge between each number pair and its least common multiple (LCM).

1. 25, 5         30

2. 7, 4          24

3. 4, 10         28

4. 16, 8         16

5. 4, 3          12

6. 3, 9          9

7. 6, 15         20

8. 12, 8         28

9. 4, 14         25

10. 6, 10        30

# Follow the directions.

You are hired to build a triangular bridge in a patch of forest that contains nine trees. The bridge can only connect three trees. How many unique triangles can you make? Explain your answer.

_____

_____

_____

# BRAINY BIRDS

African grey parrots are among the most intelligent of all animals. In fact, scientists believe they are as smart as a three- or four-year-old child. That's one intelligent bird.

One scientist who studied grey parrots raised her own, including one named Alex. Using a reward system, Alex learned many new things. By the time Alex passed away, he could count aloud to six. He knew the difference between five shapes and seven colors. He could even put things in groups by shape, color, or material. Best of all, Alex liked to teach other parrots these skills. He even scolded them if they messed up.

Grey parrots like to be helpful. They are smart enough to know when another parrot needs help and kind enough to give it. In one experiment, two grey parrots learned they would get a piece of walnut if they used their beaks to hand tokens to the scientist. In another experiment, they tested to see if one parrot would help the other get food. It worked. Each parrot was willing to give the other a token so it could get a walnut piece too. Grey parrots know how to share!

**AFRICAN GREY PARROT**

**FUN FACT** — Two boxes can be used to check a parrot's reasoning skills. One box holds a little bird food. The other holds more. Both boxes are shaken. As the parrot listens, it will choose the box with more food.

**Write a response to each question.**

1. What is the main idea of the passage?

   _____

   _____

2. Identify two key details that support the main idea.

   _____

   _____

**Match each word to its definition.**

3. intelligent                           something of value that is earned

4. reward                             something that stands for something else

5. scold                                             smart or clever

6. token                                             to speak angrily

**Match each mixed number to its equivalent improper fraction.**

1. $4\frac{1}{8}$    $\frac{17}{8}$

2. $1\frac{1}{2}$    $\frac{7}{2}$

3. $2\frac{1}{8}$    $\frac{39}{7}$

4. $3\frac{2}{3}$    $\frac{3}{2}$

5. $5\frac{4}{7}$    $\frac{11}{3}$

6. $3\frac{1}{2}$    $\frac{19}{4}$

7. $2\frac{5}{9}$    $\frac{17}{7}$

8. $4\frac{3}{4}$    $\frac{10}{3}$

9. $2\frac{3}{7}$    $\frac{23}{9}$

10. $3\frac{1}{3}$   $\frac{33}{8}$

I'M ONLY FRACTIONALLY SMARTER THAN ALEXA.

# Follow the directions.

Help Alex find the top view of each ring stacker toy. As you draw lines you will cross through the numbers. One number will be left uncrossed. Use the number to answer the question.

**Question**: For how many years did Irene care for Alex?

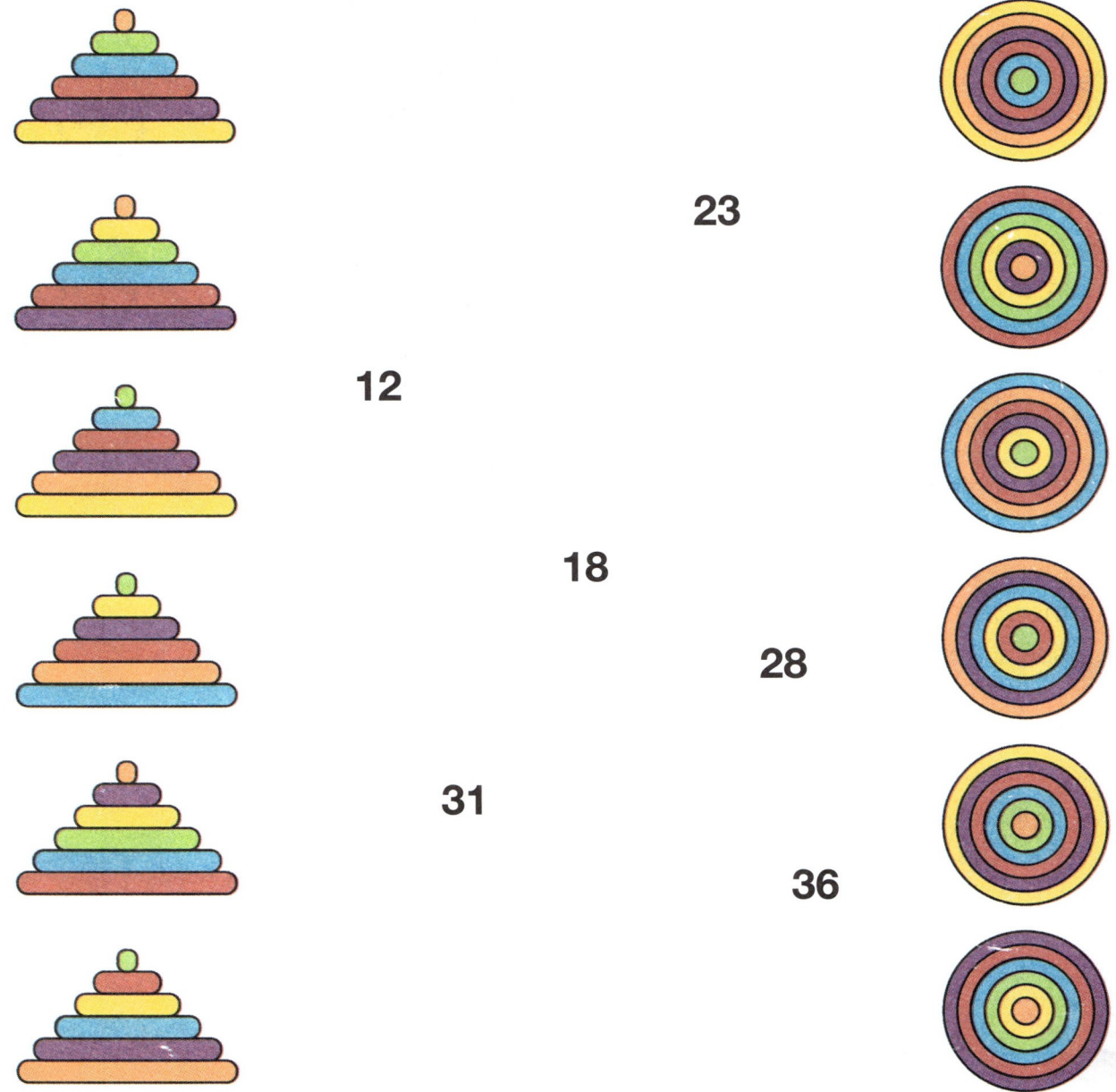

**Answer**: Irene cared for Alex for _____ years.

# A HELPING HAND

Birth defects and accidents don't happen only to people. They can happen to animals too. In the past, most animals born with congenital defects or damaged limbs did not have a positive future. Costly surgeries or euthanasia were the only options. But that has changed.

Animals, just like people, are being fitted with custom prosthetic and orthotic devices to help them live happier lives. A prosthesis, for example, replaces a missing limb. The device is worn where the limb would be. It is made of plastic and foam for a comfortable fit. It is attached with straps and buckles.

ELEPHANT WITH PROSTHETIC LEG

Most animals receiving these devices are dogs. A dog's trusting and friendly disposition makes it an excellent candidate for receiving a prosthetic device. With advances in technology, materials, and 3-D printing, most of these dogs with special needs live long and healthy lives.

One human hero named Derrick Campana is one of the world's leading experts in animal orthoses. His mission is to give disabled animals more options to live mobile lives. Campana has created devices for elephants, donkeys, ducks, cats, and of course, dogs. Although he started his career creating human prostheses and orthoses, he has always loved animals. Marrying his passion and his love is a dream come true for him.

**FUN FACT**  Even birds can be helped with prostheses. A toucan, whose beak was injured, received a 3-D printed beak. It was able to eat and sing again.

**Answer each question.**

1. What was the author's purpose in writing this passage?

    A. to inform

    B. to entertain

    C. to persuade

2. What reason does the author give that dogs are good patients for prostheses?

    A. People love dogs more than other animals.

    B. Dogs are born without limbs.

    C. Dogs have trusting and friendly personalities.

**Write the meaning of each word as it is used in the passage.**

3. device

_____

4. defect

_____

_____

## Use the table to answer each question.

A company makes prosthetic devices for approximately 100 animals each year. The percentages are below.

| horses | 23% |
|---|---|
| birds | 10% |
| reptiles | 4% |
| goats | 16% |
| dogs | 35% |
| cats | 12% |

1. About how many of the animals are goats and horses? _____

2. About how many of the animals are cats and dogs? _____

## Solve each problem.

3. Fanny's Farm has 100 rescued animals. Of these animals, 42 are goats, 14 are pigs, and the rest are cows. What percentage of the animals are cows?

   _____ cows

4. Annie's Animal Rescue has 200 animals. Of these animals, 6% are fish, 13% are reptiles, 46% are dogs, and the rest are cats. How many cats are there?

   _____ cats

# Follow the directions.

Derrick Campana first began building prostheses for humans, but one day he built his first prosthesis for a dog. The dog was born with limb deformities.

To answer the question, begin by crossing out the name *Rex*. Move counterclockwise around the circle crossing out every other name you come across. Remember that once you have crossed out a name, you do not count that name as you go around the circle. Write the remaining name on the line.

**Question**: What was the dog's name?

**Answer**: The dog's name was _____ .

# LIZARDS FIGHT BACK

Animals have many ways to protect themselves from their enemies. These are called defense mechanisms. They help animals stay alive.

Horned lizards have excellent defense mechanisms. These small reptiles live in North American deserts. They have scary predators that are much bigger, such as hawks, coyotes, dogs, and snakes. So, how does a small horned lizard protect itself from a big, hungry coyote?

It shoots blood at it from its eye! The blood can spurt as far as four feet (122 cm). When the horned lizard sees danger, its blood pressure rises. Blood gathers in a sac below its eyes. It tries to squirt the blood into the predator's mouth, hoping the taste alone will scare it off. It tastes awful.

Blood-squirting is the horned lizard's last resort in fighting off predators. It has other moves. It starts by hissing and lunging. If that doesn't work, it can inflate to nearly double its size. It might also flatten itself to look like a pile of pebbles. When all else fails, it uses its best defense—projectile bleeding. Horned lizards are good at looking out for themselves!

HORNED LIZARD

**FUN FACT**

Other creatures, including some snakes and insects, release blood to protect themselves. The armored cricket is one. It shoots blood from seams in its exoskeleton.

**Circle the answer that is NOT a meaning for each word or phrase.**

1. defense mechanism

    A. a part of the US army

    B. a way a creature protects itself

    C. a way to survive

2. projectile

    A. something shooting out quickly

    B. something poisonous

    C. something flying out with great force

**Write F for *fact* or O for *opinion*.**

_____ 3. Horned lizards have excellent defense mechanisms.

_____ 4. Its blood can spurt as far as four feet (122 cm).

_____ 5. The horned lizard's blood tastes awful.

_____ 6. It starts by hissing and lunging.

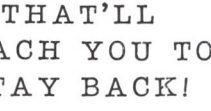

THAT'LL TEACH YOU TO STAY BACK!

**Solve each problem.**

1. Harry the horned lizard shoots blood from his eye at three predators in one day. If he shoots out blood at lengths of 122 cm on average per animal, how many meters in all did he shoot?

   _____ m

2. Hilda the horned lizard spurts a total length of 3.5 feet of blood at a predator. How many inches did she spurt?

   _____ in.

**Use the figure to answer each question.**

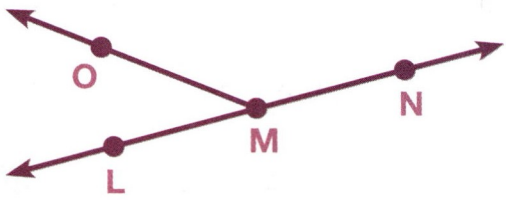

3. Name four points. _____ _____

   _____ _____

4. Name two line segments. _____ _____

5. Name three rays. _____ _____

   _____

6. Name a line. _____

**Follow the directions.**

Use a ruler to draw a line (from dot to dot) from the lizard to each of its predators. Use scale to measure the lines and answer the question.

**Question:** Which animal is 105 cm away from the horned lizard?

**Scale: 1 mm = 1cm**

HORNED LIZARD

SNAKE

HAWK

COYOTE

**Answer:** The _____ is 105 cm away from the lizard.

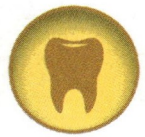
# NO SWEET TOOTH HERE

Do you crave endless amounts of sweets day after day? Well, that craving for sweets is part of most mammals' survival. Sweet signals the presence of carbohydrates, or the nutrients that give a body energy. But some mammals cannot taste sweet.

You may have heard the words herbivore, carnivore, and omnivore—the three animal categories that are based on what animals eat. An herbivore eats mostly plants. A carnivore eats mostly meats. And an omnivore eats both plants and meat. Well, cats, who are carnivores, do not taste sweet in the same way we do.

It's all about genes and DNA. Not the jeans that you wear, but the genes you are born with. Human tongues have taste receptor cells that taste things that are sweet, bitter, salty, sour, and umami (savory). Scientists have conducted studies testing which taste receptors mammals have. Cats are the only ones lacking the sweet gene.

What does this mean for your beloved Fluffy? If your four-legged, purr-fect companion has a taste for ice cream or candy, it's not because they enjoy the sweetness of it like you do. They may be detecting something else in the taste. Check your pet's food. Too often, pet food companies include corn products in their cat food. We know it is not to make the food taste better to cats, so avoid the unnecessary ingredients and allow your cat to live a long and healthy life. And save the sweet stuff for you.

 **FUN FACT** — Did you know that you taste things with not only your tongue, but also with the back of your throat, epiglottis, nose, sinuses, lips, and cheeks?

**Complete each sentence with a word from the word bank.**

| plants | gene | survival | carnivore |

1. A sweet craving is part of a human's _____.

2. Herbivores eat diets rich in _____.

3. Cats lack the _____ that allows them to taste things that are sweet.

4. A _____ eats a diet rich in meat.

**Write two different meanings for each word. Include the parts of speech.**

5. sense

_____

_____

6. plant

_____

_____

7. taste

_____

_____

SHHH! DO-NUT TELL ANYONE!

**Solve each problem.**

1. There are five members of the Sweet family. If each person has 1,716 tastebuds, how many tastebuds do they have in all?

   _____ tastebuds

2. The Umami family members each have 3,428 tastebuds. If there are four family members, how many tastebuds do they have in all?

   _____ tastebuds

3. The Bitter family has a total of 6,027 tastebuds. If three family members have the same number of tastebuds, how many do they each have?

   _____ tastebuds

4. The Sour family adopts two kittens. Together, the kittens have 940 tastebuds. If each kitten has the same number of tastebuds, how many do they each have?

   _____ tastebuds

**Follow the directions.**

You look out your window and see 5 cats. There are 2 black cats, 1 orange cat, 1 gray cat, and 1 white cat. Read the clues and color the cats.

- There are two cats of different colors between the gray cat and the orange cat.

- The orange cat is the only cat between the black cats.

- The gray cat is on the right.

# THE LOOK-ALIKES

It's often easy to figure out how some insects get their names. What do you call a red-and-black insect with a neck so long it looks like a giraffe? A giraffe weevil, of course. Like giraffes, this weevil uses its long neck to fight other male giraffe weevils. Another look-alike is the rhinoceros beetle. It has a long horn on its head that can be up to 6 inches (15 cm) long. They are popular pets in parts of Asia.

GIRAFFE WEEVIL

Insects aren't the only ones named after other animals. The elephant shrew is small, compared to its namesake, but it has a long nose just like an elephant's trunk. It uses its nose to locate food. A bee hummingbird is almost as small as a large bee and weighs less than a penny. Leopard frogs are covered in spots like the jungle cat.

Some animal names are misleading. The camel spider is not a spider or a camel, but it enjoys the shade a camel makes in the hot desert. A red panda is not even remotely related to its black and white bear namesake. And don't get me started on starfish, seahorse, guinea pig and flying fox—all of which are NOT related to their namesakes. So, whether an animal looks like or acts like another, using common animal names can be fun, but confusing.

RHINOCEROS BEETLE

 **FUN FACT** Some animals have evolved to look like other things to keep them safe. An owl butterfly gets its name from the huge eyespots on their wings. This scares a predator into thinking it is a much bigger creature.

**Match each animal to its identifying body part.**

1. giraffe weevil                                    long horn on head

2. rhinoceros beetle                                 long nose

3. elephant shrew                                    spots

4. leopard frog                                      long neck

**Write a response to each question.**

5. What does the word *namesake* mean as it is used in the passage?

_____

_____

6. Why does the author say that some animal names are *misleading*? Support your answer with evidence from the text.

_____

_____

_____

_____

_____

Use the figure to answer each question.

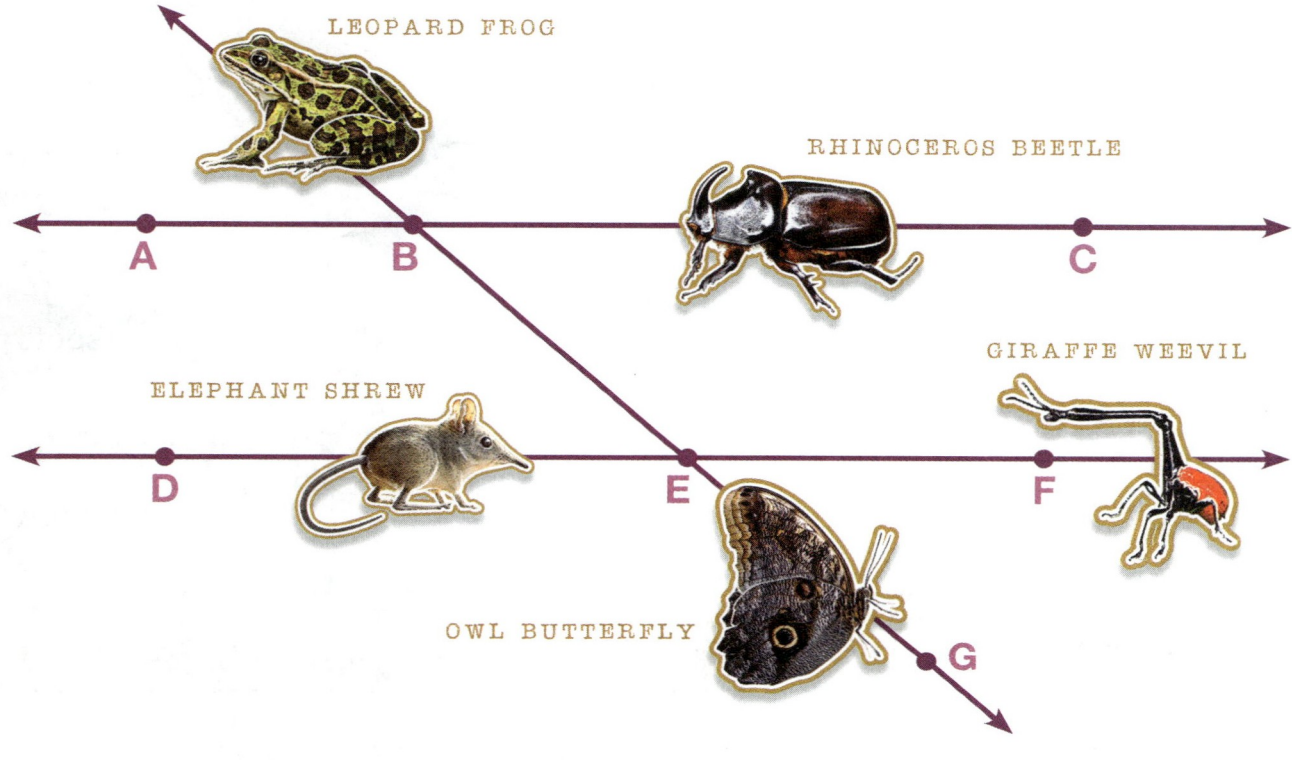

1. Which animal is on line $\overleftrightarrow{AC}$? _____

2. Which animal is closest to point F? _____

3. Which animals are on parallel lines? _____

4. Which animal is between points E and G? _____

5. Name two points of intersection. _____

**Draw the lines.**

6. Perpendicular lines $\overleftrightarrow{HJ}$ and $\overleftrightarrow{KL}$ intersecting at point M.

**Follow the directions.**

Imagine you are tasked with coming up with a new animal whose attributes resemble those of other animals. Draw a picture of your new creature and write a paragraph describing its appearance, behavior, and habitat. You can borrow traits from any other animal.

_____

_____

_____

_____

_____

_____

_____

# DEAD OR ALIVE?

Why would anyone use a word that means "dead body" to name a beautiful flower? Someone did. The *titan arum* is also known as a corpse flower. It's called a corpse flower because it smells like rotting meat. You may have smelled a dead mouse in your basement or a rotting fish at the beach. It's the worst smell ever, right? So maybe you don't want to smell a corpse flower! Don't worry. You're not likely to get sick from smelling a corpse flower. It's gross, but fortunately the smell doesn't last long.

The dark reddish purple corpse flower is the largest and smelliest flower in the plant world. It grows up to 10 feet (3 m) tall and takes seven to ten years to bloom. When it blooms, it stinks for about 48 hours.

This flower's odor is important to the plant. To reproduce, it needs to attract carrion beetles and flesh flies. These insects are attracted to the smell of rotting meat. That's where they like to lay their eggs. As they lay their eggs, they become covered in pollen and carry it off to unknowingly pollinate another corpse flower.

CORPSE FLOWER

In 2015, 75,000 people visited the Chicago Botanic Garden to see its first corpse flower, named Spike, bloom. Sadly, Spike never got the energy to open. What rotten luck.

**Write a response to each question.**

1. How did the author help you infer the meaning of the word *corpse*?

   _____

   _____

2. How might the corpse flower's odor help attract insects?

   _____

   _____

**Match each adjective to the noun as it is used in the text.**

3. rotting                    flower

4. smelliest                  mouse

5. dead                       meat

EWWWWW!

## Use the data to create a line graph showing each flower's growth.

A botanical garden measured the heights of two of its corpse flowers.

| Corpse Flower Bloom #1 Height | |
|---|---|
| Day 1 | 53 in. |
| Day 3 | 61 in. |
| Day 5 | 72 in. |
| Day 7 | 80.5 in. |
| Day 9 | 88 in. |
| Day 11 | 97 in. |

| Corpse Flower Bloom #2 Height | |
|---|---|
| Day 1 | 50 in. |
| Day 2 | 54 in. |
| Day 3 | 62 in. |
| Day 4 | 67.5 in. |
| Day 5 | 72 in. |
| Day 6 | 79 in. |
| Day 7 | 84.5 in. |
| Day 8 | 89.5 in. |
| Day 9 | 94.5 in. |
| Day 10 | 95.5 in. |
| Day 11 | 97.5 in. |

■ Corpse Flower Bloom #1
■ Corpse Flower Bloom #2

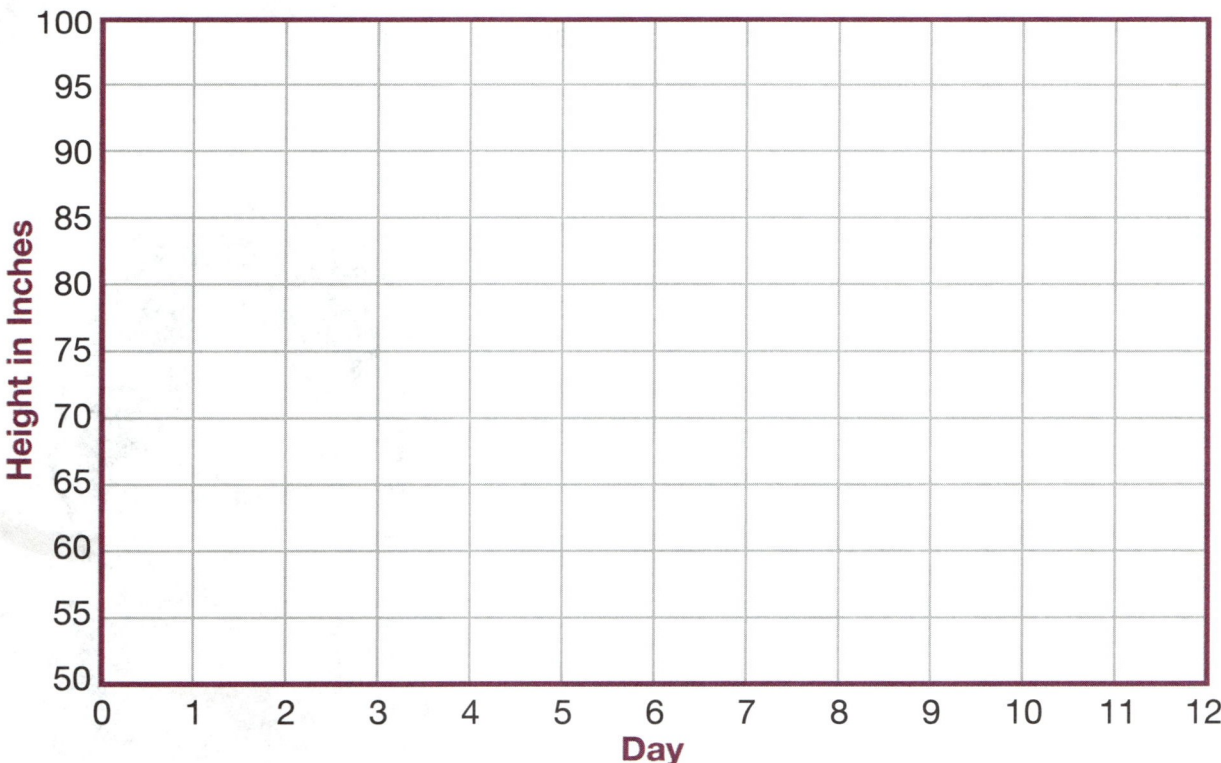

1. On which day did each flower have the same height? _____

2. Which bloom grew the most from Day 1 to Day 11? _____

**Follow the directions.**

Use only even digits (include 0) to complete each equation.

1. _____ + _____ + _____ = 2

2. _____ + _____ + _____ = 16

3. _____ + _____ + _____ = 20

4. _____ + _____ + _____ = 18

5. _____ + _____ + _____ = 12

6. _____ + _____ + _____ = 24

Use digits that are less than 6 to complete each equation.

7. _____ × _____ × _____ = 6

8. _____ × _____ × _____ = 12

9. _____ × _____ × _____ = 10

10. _____ × _____ × _____ = 20

# BATHROOM BUDDIES

The ancient Romans have done a lot to influence modern society. This includes the use of toilets. Roman men and women used public toilets, sometimes at the same time. These ancient toilets were long, white marble benches with holes in them. Yes, you sat over the hole. The benches were built above stone-lined gutters filled with water. Snakes and rats sometimes hung out there. Yikes!

ANCIENT ROMAN PUBLIC TOILETS

In each of these restrooms was a sea sponge on a stick. People used the sponge to clean themselves after they pooped. The sponge was dipped in water and then used to rinse off one's backside. What else were they to do? They had no toilet paper then. But wait, it gets worse. These sticks were shared. By everyone!

At home, Romans peed into small pots. They were for urine only. When full, the pots were dumped into a big pee jar down the street. Once a week, the pee jars were carried to a laundry where the pee was poured onto dirty clothes. Did you know that urine is good for getting out stubborn stains? I wouldn't try this at home if I were you.

 In ancient Roman times, you had no sponge-on-a-stick tool in your toilet if you were poor. Instead, you cleaned up with small stones.

**Complete each sentence with a word from the word bank.**

| ancient | public | sponge | urine |

1. A _____ on a stick was used instead of toilet paper.

2. Many Roman bathrooms were _____ and used by everyone.

3. The _____ Romans had unusual bathroom habits.

4. Many Romans collected their _____ to clean their clothes.

**Write a response to the question.**

5. Write an opinion about ancient Roman toilets. Support your opinion with at least two reasons.

_____

_____

_____

_____

I THINK I'LL HOLD IT.

**Find the volume of each structure. Each unit is 1 cubic meter.**

The ancient Romans were great builders of their time. They used mathematical equations to design and build their structures. To find the volume, multiply length x width x height.

1.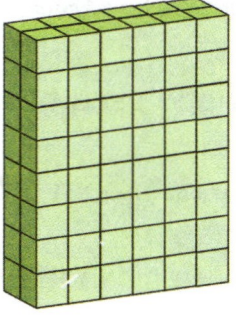

_____ m³

2.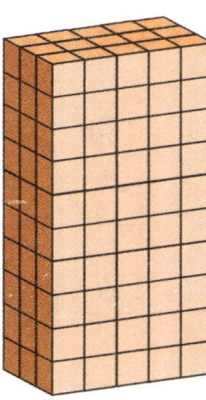

_____ m³

3.

_____ m³

4.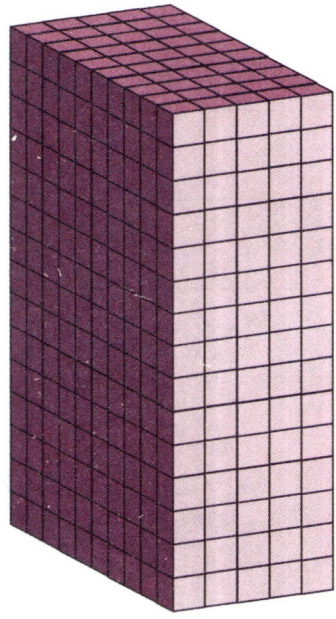

_____ m³

**Follow the directions.**

The ancient Romans invented much of what we use today. Find the names of 10 inventions in the puzzle.

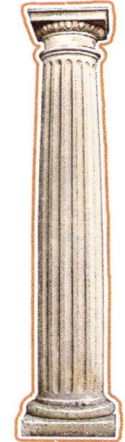

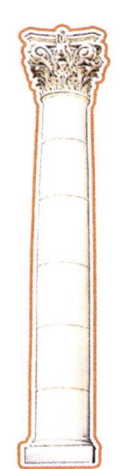

SEWER

HIGHWAY

AQUEDUCT

CALENDAR

NEWSPAPER

CONCRETE

ROMAN NUMERALS

ARCHES

BOUND BOOK

POSTAL SERVICE

```
R P W D T S M J H L K B G O H
C O N C R E T E M O K L D S I
R S M T Z W B V O L G C H Y G
J T H A E E N B R Y U A Q X H
T A H G N R D E J N V L G S W
D L G U I N A B W N M E J K A
F S G H U J U Y C S K N O K Y
Q E T O S D F M G H P D J K L
E R B R A R C H E S T A Y U J
U V I S D G V B M R T R P F H
L I D F G H J K L Y A P U E C
Q C W N I L U T Y O V L G X R
S E D A Q U E D U C T H S L K
```

# BEWARE OF ALLIGATOR

You surely have heard of John Quincy Adams. He was the sixth president of the United States, from 1825 to 1829. But, you may not know about his pet alligator. It is said to have lived with President Adams in the White House.

The story goes that in 1825, President Adams had a visit from French war hero, Marquis de Lafayette. Lafayette did not come empty-handed. He had been given an alligator as a gift on his tour of the 24 states in America. He regifted the alligator to President Adams. What do you do when a famous person gives you an alligator? President Adams kept the alligator in a bathtub in the East Room. The room was unfinished at the time and was a safe place to keep an alligator. The president often gave tours without warning visitors about his unusual pet. Guests understandably freaked out when they came upon one of North America's largest reptiles!

John Quincy Adams was not the only president to keep an alligator in the White House. President Herbert Hoover's son owned two pet alligators.

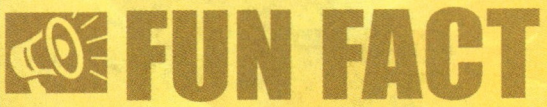 **FUN FACT** President Lincoln had pet goats in the White House. Their names were Nanny and Nanko. Other unusual White House pets included donkeys, roosters, and bears.

**Answer each question.**

1. Why did the Marquis de Lafayette give President Adams an alligator?

    A. He knew alligators were popular pets in the new country.

    B. He had been told alligators were good to eat.

    C. Someone gave him an alligator, so he passed it on.

2. Which other president kept pet alligators at the White House?

    A. President Obama

    B. President Hoover

    C. President Lincoln

**Write a response to each question.**

3. How would this story be different if President Adams had been given a kitten?
___
___

4. Would you want an alligator as a pet? Why or why not?
___
___
___

**Compare each pair of expressions. Circle the one that is greater.**

1. $2.5 \times 0.11 - 0.09$        $2.5 \times (0.11 - 0.09)$

2. $1.3 + 2.6 \div 0.02$        $(1.3 + 2.6) \div 0.02$

3. $4 \times \frac{1}{2} + \frac{1}{8}$        $4 \times (\frac{1}{2} + \frac{1}{8})$

4. $7.2 \div (0.8 - 0.2)$        $7.2 \div 0.8 - 0.2$

RUB-A-DUB-DUB, 1 ALLIGATOR IN A TUB!

**Write an expression for each problem.**

5. Jessie biked $3\frac{3}{4}$ mile on Monday and $3\frac{3}{4}$ mile on Tuesday. On Wednesday, she biked three times as much as Monday and Tuesday combined.

6. Ty has $\frac{1}{8}$ pound of turkey and $\frac{1}{6}$ pound of ham on each sandwich. He has 5 sandwiches.

# Follow the directions.

Help the guests flee from the alligator! Draw a line through a path where each fraction is greater than the one before it.

START

$\frac{1}{12}$  $\frac{1}{10}$  $\frac{2}{12}$

$\frac{6}{12}$  $\frac{5}{12}$  $\frac{4}{12}$  $\frac{1}{8}$  $\frac{3}{12}$

$\frac{1}{12}$  $\frac{1}{3}$  $\frac{1}{4}$  $\frac{1}{6}$  $\frac{2}{10}$  $\frac{6}{12}$

$\frac{1}{2}$  $\frac{3}{10}$  $\frac{4}{10}$  $\frac{5}{10}$  $\frac{1}{10}$  $\frac{2}{8}$

$\frac{7}{12}$  $\frac{3}{4}$  $\frac{3}{8}$  $\frac{1}{8}$  $\frac{1}{6}$

$\frac{8}{10}$  $\frac{5}{6}$

FINISH

# A BIRTHDAY BITE

Every part of the world has birthday traditions. Many people get gifts, go out to dinner, or take special trips. Almost everyone gets a cake for their birthday, complete with candles. You know the rest of the story. You make a wish and blow out the candles, right?

In Mexico, they take it one step further. The birthday boy or girl's face gets smashed into the cake! This custom is called *la mordida* in Spanish. At birthday parties, it is slang for "take a bite." Instead of singing a birthday song while the candles are blown out, family and friends yell, "Mordida! Mordida! Mordida!"

## FUN FACT

Other cake-smashing traditions include one from the ancient Romans. A wedding cake was smashed over the bride's head to bring lots of children.

*WAIT! HOW MANY CHILDREN!?*

At that sound, the birthday boy or girl is supposed to lean down and take a bite of the cake without using their hands. Just as they touch their mouths to the yummy cake—smash! Someone pushes their face into the creamy icing of the birthday cake. It's hard then to tell which has more icing, the cake or the face of the birthday boy or girl!

**Number the sentences from 1 to 3 to show the order of events.**

_____ 1. Someone pushes the birthday boy or girl's face into the cake.

_____ 2. The birthday boy or girl leans down to bite the cake.

_____ 3. Family and friends shout, "Mordida!"

**Match each word to its definition.**

4. tradition              take a bite, in Spanish

5. la mordida             the usual way of behaving

6. slang                  a popular way to say something

**Color the three numbers that when multiplied equal the top given number.**

1. 72

| 6 | 3 |
|---|---|
| 4 | 5 |

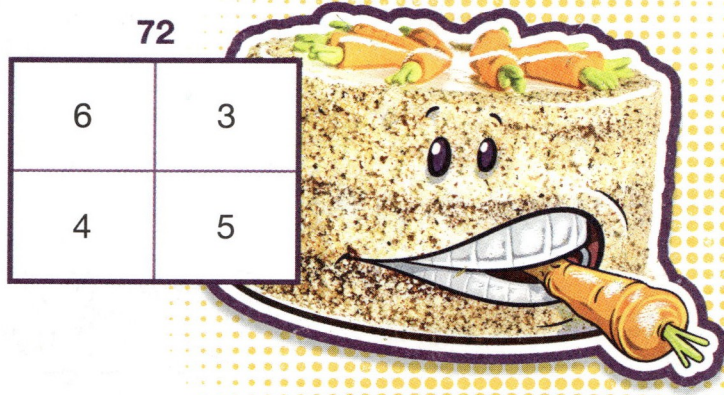

2. 168

| 4 | 7 |
|---|---|
| 6 | 2 |

3. 180

| 8 | 9 |
|---|---|
| 5 | 4 |

4. 240

| 5 | 6 |
|---|---|
| 7 | 8 |

# Follow the directions.

Solve each expression. To answer the question, write the letters of the correct answers in order on the lines.

**Question**: In what country do children get to officially skip chores and homework on their birthdays?

1. $\frac{1}{10}$ of 764

| 7.64 | 76.4 |
|---|---|
| G | H |

2. 1,000 times greater than 2.7

| 27,000 | 2,700 |
|---|---|
| U | E |

3. $\frac{1}{100}$ of 4,590

| 45.9 | 459 |
|---|---|
| R | N |

4. 10 times greater than 0.68

| 68 | 6.8 |
|---|---|
| M | G |

5. 0.01 times smaller than 5,830

| 58.3 | 583 |
|---|---|
| A | E |

6. 1,000 times smaller than 431

| 4.31 | 0.431 |
|---|---|
| R | N |

7. $\frac{1}{10}$ of 9.57

| 0.957 | 0.0957 |
|---|---|
| Y | S |

**Answer**: __ __ __ __ __ __ __

UNUSUALLY FUN READING & MATH GRADE 5   71

# BARF BAGS

People collect anything, from baseball cards to comic books to vomit bags. Whoa. Vomit bags? Yes! Some collectors hunt far and wide for one more vomit bag. They find them on airplanes, in hospitals, or even on eBay! Hopefully, they're the ones that say, "Never used!"

Niek Vermeulen is a Dutch collector whose collection could make you sick! He earned a world record with 6,016 vomit sacks from 1,142 airlines in 160 countries. He began collecting air-sickness bags on a bet with a friend.

Barf bags are collectible because there are so many kinds. The Eastern Airlines vomit sack is pretty, with white flowers. A friendly airplane face smiles on the Cebu Pacific Air barf bag and reads, *Save the Earth. Use this bag only when necessary.* Kuwait Airways' throw-up sack shows a bird with its beak held high. This airline is no longer flying, so its barf bags are in high demand.

Visit a virtual museum of barf bags! Search online for *Air Sickness Bag Museum*. At present, the collector has 3,278 bags. Check to see if he's gotten more recently. If you see a bag you like in the collection, the owner may be willing to trade with you!

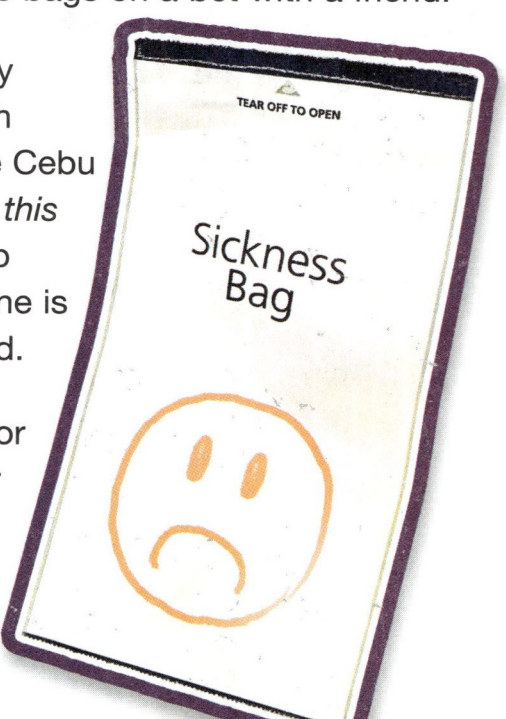

## FUN FACT

Other interesting collections around the world include plastic ducks, *Do Not Disturb* signs, celebrity hair, and hamburgers. And then there are gross collections such as dried-up poo and toe-nail clippings. Bleh.

**Write F for *fact* or O for *opinion*.**

_____ 1. People collect anything from baseball cards to comic books.

_____ 2. Niek Vermeulen's collection might make you sick.

_____ 3. The Eastern Airlines vomit sack is pretty.

_____ 4. You can visit an online Air Sickness Bag Museum.

**Write an antonym for each word or phrase.**

5. collect _____

6. in demand _____

**Write a response to the question.**

7. What do you collect? Tell about your collection and draw a picture.

_____

_____

**Solve each row of problems.**

1. 40 ÷ 10 = _____     76 ÷ 10 = _____     3.2 ÷ 10 = _____

2. 40 ÷ 100 = _____    76 ÷ 100 = _____    3.2 ÷ 100 = _____

3. 40 ÷ 1,000 = _____  76 ÷ 1,000 = _____  3.2 ÷ 1,000 = _____

**Match each problem to its answer.**

4. 3000 ÷ 10 =           0.003

5. 0.3 ÷ 10 =            3

6. 30 ÷ 100 =            300

7. 3 ÷ 1,000 =           0.03

8. 30 ÷ 10 =             0.3

WE'RE IN FOR A BUMPY RIDE!

## Follow the directions.

On a long and bumpy flight, one passenger approaches a flight attendant to say that she is going to be sick. The flight attendant quickly retrieves a bag and turns to hand it to the passenger, but the passenger has returned to her seat. The flight attendant looks around. She sees all the rows filled with an odd number of passengers. Some nearby passengers tell the flight attendant where the sick passenger is.

- "She is sitting in the third row."

- "She is sitting in the fourth row from the back."

- "She is sitting in the second seat from the right."

- "She is sitting in the fourth seat from the left."

**Question**: How many people are on the plane?
(Hint: draw a diagram to help you.)

**Answer**: There are _____ passengers on the plane.

# SMASH BASH

Superstitions are everywhere. Many superstitions warn people against doing something that will bring them bad luck such as, don't walk under a ladder, don't break a mirror, and don't open an umbrella inside. Other people may choose to believe that something will bring them wealth, good health, or good luck.

In Germany, brides and grooms believe broken plates and cups will bring them a happy marriage. The night before a wedding, guests are invited to a party. It's called a *polterabend*, German for "noisy evening." The party is usually outside. Guests enjoy food, music, and dancing. But, they mostly enjoy breaking things! Guests show up with boxes of dinnerware. As the crowd gets worked up, they take turns smashing cups and plates to the ground. And, you just might see a toilet bowl or bathtub thrown in the mix!

The engaged couple stands by with brooms, ready to clean up the mess. The hope is that this teaches them to work together during their marriage.

**FUN FACT** — In South Korea, a groom's ankles are tied together and the soles of his feet are beaten with a dead fish. This tradition is said to test the groom's strength of character.

I HATE WEDDINGS.

**Answer each question.**

1. Which is NOT a superstition?

    A. Don't walk under ladders.

    B. Brush your teeth to avoid cavities.

    C. Black cats bring bad luck.

2. Why do couples sweep up the smashed dinnerware together at a *polterabend*?

    A. to see if they truly love each other

    B. to prove they are a good match

    C. to learn to work together

**Write five compound words from the text.**

3. _____

4. _____

5. _____

6. _____

7. _____

**Write a response to the question.**

8. What is your opinion about the wedding tradition of a *polterabend*? Explain.

_____

_____

_____

**Solve each problem.**

1. At Heidi and Heinrich's *polterabend* a total of 84 plates were smashed. The couple swept up 672 pieces. Into about how many pieces did each plate break?

   _____ pieces

2. At Ingrid and Dieter's *polterabend* there were 952 pieces to sweep up. Using the answer from #1, about how many plates were smashed?

   _____ plates

**Use long division to solve each row of problems.**

3. 7)133          4)316          8)496

4. 13)832        25)375        19)2,793

**Match each plate to its broken piece.**

# FOOD FIGHT

The world's most famous food fight takes place each year at the end of August in the small town of Buñol, Spain. During the La Tomatina Festival, more than 20,000 merrymakers pick up tomatoes and paint the town red.

The festival started in the 1940s during a parade. Villagers remember some kids horsing around, making one of the parade figures' headpiece fall. A fight broke out. Bystanders grabbed tomatoes from a nearby vegetable stand and started throwing them. Splat!

No one forgot the tomato fight. The next year, parade goers even brought tomatoes from home. As the parade marched on, they started flinging tomatoes right and left. Soon, the streets—and people—were a red mess of tomato pulp and seeds.

Each year during La Tomatina Festival, the narrow streets of Buñol fill with 22,000 partygoers pelting each other with more than 140 tons (127 metric tons) of ripe tomatoes. The tomato throwing lasts for one hour, after which a shot goes off signaling the end of the fight. The largest food fight in the world is done for another year!

Due to the huge number of people who visit the festival, the town sells tickets so that no more than 22,000 tomato throwers attend. Get your ticket ahead of time. And bring tomatoes!

**Answer each question.**

1. Which did NOT happen at the first food fight in Buñol, Spain?

   A. Kids started horsing around with a parade figure.

   B. Bystanders started throwing tomatoes from a vegetable stand.

   C. A parade figure threw tomatoes at the crowd.

2. How did the food fight become a festival?

   A. Villagers remembered the tomato fight as a fun time.

   B. The town grows so many tomatoes they go to waste.

   C. People from all over visit the town every year.

**Write a synonym for each word from the passage.**

3. village _____

4. fling _____

5. partygoers _____

**Write a response to the question.**

6. How did the first food fight differ from the food fight it is today?

_____

_____

**Solve each problem.**

1. Last year, the festival sold 22,000 tickets. If each of those 22,000 people bring 20 tomatoes, how many tomatoes would be at the festival in all?

   _____ tomatoes

2. The previous year the festival sold only 20,880 tickets and brought in 313,200 pounds of tomatoes. About how many pounds would each person get?

   _____ pounds

3. It takes 12 fire trucks to hose down the streets of Buñol after the festival is done. If each fire truck carries 750 gallons of water, how much water do they use in all?

   _____ gallons

**Complete the chart.**

4. After the festival many roads were blocked off to clean the buildings pelted with tomatoes. Use the data to figure out the average number of tomatoes per building.

| Road | Number of tomatoes | Number of buildings | Number of tomatoes per building |
|---|---|---|---|
| Calle del Sol | 1,872 | 12 | |
| Calle de Utiel | 3,264 | 16 | |
| Calle de Chiva | 1,110 | 15 | |

**Follow the directions.**

Pablo and Sofía have a huge bucket of tomatoes they are bringing to the festival. They each decide to stack the tomatoes in pyramids. Pablo decides to make a triangular base with 6 tomatoes along each side. Sofía decides to make a square base with 5 tomatoes on each side. Pablo and Sofía continue stacking tomatoes until they each have only 1 at the top.

**Question**: Who uses the most tomatoes to build their pyramid and how many tomatoes did they use?

Draw a picture or describe how you solved for the answer.

**Answer**: _____ used _____ tomatoes.

# CELEBRATE THIS!

May 29 is *Put a Pillow on Your Fridge Day*. Who celebrates pillows on refrigerators? Anyone looking for wealth and good luck—that's who!

No one knows the exact origin of this holiday, but it may have come from a time when people didn't have refrigerators. Some homes had larders. Larders were cool areas or rooms where raw meat was covered in lard, or animal fat. The fat would preserve the meat. By the 1700s people kept other perishable foods in the larder too.

The story goes that people would put linens in their larder one day each year. They believed that this would bring luck to their household. It may have just made their linens smell like last night's dinner, but nonetheless, a tradition began.

As larders were replaced by refrigerators, the tradition evolved. Putting a pillow on your fridge is the new way to celebrate this day in May.

There are so many other unusual holidays to celebrate. Check out the list on the fridge and mark your calendars. You don't want to miss out on the fun!

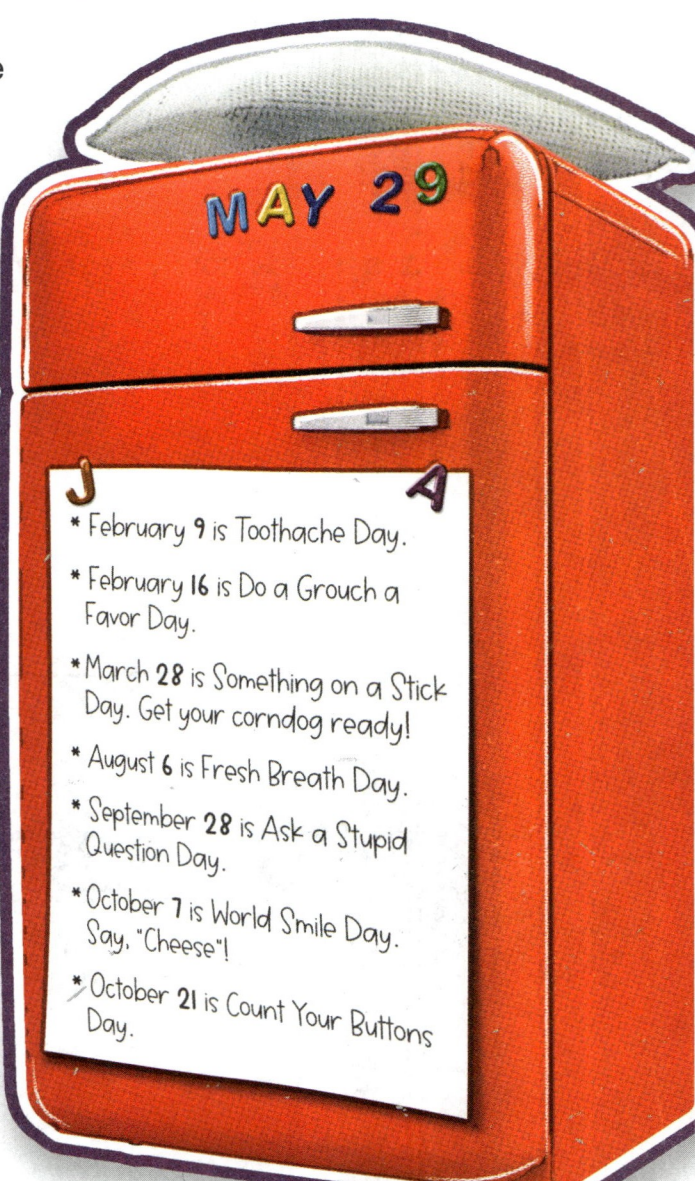

* February 9 is Toothache Day.
* February 16 is Do a Grouch a Favor Day.
* March 28 is Something on a Stick Day. Get your corndog ready!
* August 6 is Fresh Breath Day.
* September 28 is Ask a Stupid Question Day.
* October 7 is World Smile Day. Say, "Cheese"!
* October 21 is Count Your Buttons Day.

Perhaps one holiday you know nothing about is celebrated on January 16. It's called *Nothing Day*. What do you do on Nothing Day? That's easy—nothing!

**Match each holiday to the date it is celebrated.**

1. World Smile Day                                    January 16

2. Put a Pillow on Your Fridge Day                    May 29

3. Count Your Buttons Day                             October 7

4. Nothing Day                                        October 21

**Answer each question.**

5. Which is NOT a definition of holiday?

    A. a day people do not go to work

    B. a day when people get married

    C. a day to celebrate a person or event

    D. a day off from school

6. Which is the best meaning of the word *origin*?

    A. beginning

    B. middle

    C. end

    D. idea

**Complete each table.**

You go to the store to shop for some items for the upcoming holidays. Calculate the change from $5 and $10 for each item.

|  | Change from $5.00 | Change from $10.00 |
|---|---|---|
| jar of buttons $1.30 |  |  |
| corn dog $2.77 |  |  |
| toothpaste & toothbrush $4.25 |  |  |

You go to the store to shop for pillows. Calculate the change from $10 and $20 for each item.

|  | Change from $10.00 | Change from $20.00 |
|---|---|---|
| throw pillow $4.98 |  |  |
| standard pillow $7.65 |  |  |
| king-size pillow $8.89 |  |  |

# Follow the directions.

Figure out the value of each object. Solve the last problem.

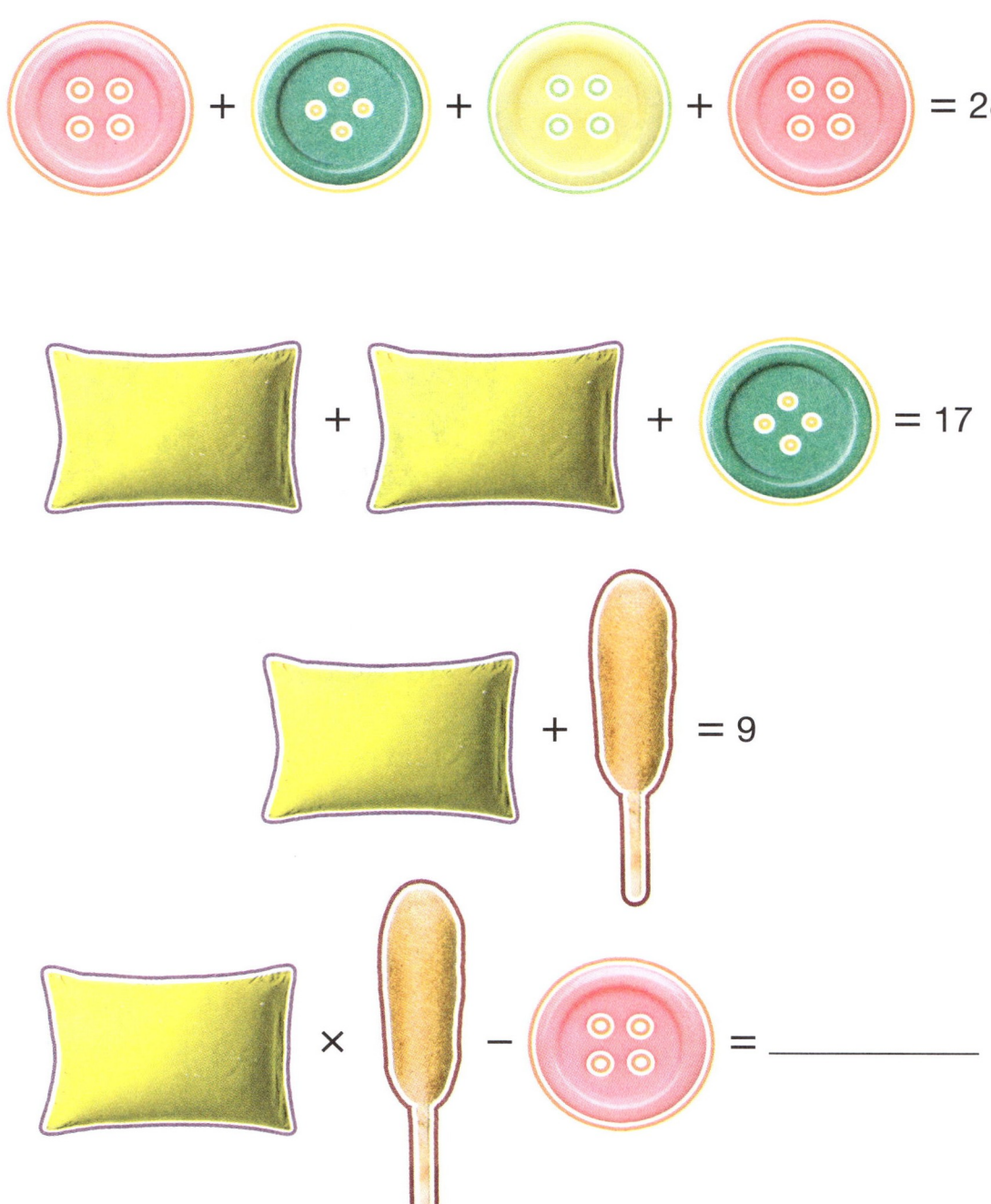

# TRICK OR TURKEY

Once, Thanksgiving and Halloween looked a lot alike. Until about 90 years ago, young and old merrymakers dressed up at Thanksgiving. No, they didn't go as turkeys!

They dressed up as just about everything else, though. Everyone got in on it, especially in New York City. People remember costumed children and grownups at every street corner on Thanksgiving Day. The most popular masks were heads of parrots or other colorful birds and animals. People wore larger than life fake heads, hands, and feet. And others dressed in disguises such as clowns, or sailors.

The streets were full of color and noise. People celebrated everywhere, some on bikes and others on horses. Partygoers blew horns and shook rattles. They threw showers of confetti and even flour. Some cities held big parades. One famous parade was the Ragamuffin Parade. Children dressed in old clothes, usually too big for them. Neighbors and people on the streets handed out treats of candy and other food or small coins.

It is not clear how the tradition of dressing up moved to Halloween, but the children who celebrate these holidays are glad that one thing stayed the same—the treats.

A TURKEY FLOAT AT THE MACY'S THANKSGIVING DAY PARADE

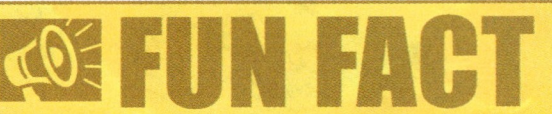

**FUN FACT**

In the 1950s, the tradition of masks and costumes turned into something equally playful and magical—the Macy's Thanksgiving Day Parade. You can still watch it in person in New York City or on TV.

**Complete each sentence with a word from the word bank.**

| confetti | disguised | merrymakers |
|---|---|---|

1. The _____ were having so much fun dressing up!

2. People love to throw _____ at parades.

3. Some people in costume were _____ as clowns.

**Write an antonym for each word from the text.**

4. remember _____

5. popular _____

**Write a response to the question.**

6. Why do you think dressing up in costume became more popular at Halloween than at Thanksgiving? Explain. Then, draw your ultimate costume!

_____

_____

_____

_____

_____

**Solve each problem. Write the remainder.**

1. 55 candies are shared amongst 6 children. How many pieces of candy will each child receive? How many are left?

   _____ pieces

2. 96 candies are shared amongst 9 children. How many pieces of candy will each child receive? How many are left?

   _____ pieces

**Solve each problem. Write the remainder as a fraction.**

3. Mrs. Grady gave 6 children 15 apples. How many apples will each child get?

   _____ apples

4. Dad peeled 17 oranges for my three siblings and me. How many oranges did we each get?

   _____ oranges

**Solve each problem. Write the remainder as a decimal.**

5. Casey earned $22 for washing windows this month. If she washed windows on five houses, how much did she charge for each house?

   $ _____

6. Eight bags of confetti cost $9.60. How much is one bag of confetti?

   $ _____

**Follow the directions to answer the question.**

Trick-or-Treating is almost over for the night and you decide to give the next child who comes to the door the rest of your candy. You have less than 20 candies left in the bowl. *Ding-dong!* Two kids are at the door. Then another is behind them. Wait! There's four total! You divide the candies amongst them equally, but you still have one candy left.

**Question**: How many candies did you have in the bowl to share? Use pictures, numbers, or other strategy to solve the problem.

**Answer**: You have _____ candies.

# DRESS IN STYLE

Clothing styles change over time. Look through your grandparents' photo albums to see how differently they dressed as kids. What do you notice?

About 100 years ago, boys wore dresses until at least age four. Pants had no zippers or snaps and were hard to open. Little boys couldn't wait for their first pair of pants. The occasion was celebrated with a small party. Boys received gifts and best of all—a pair of pants.

Little girls always wore dresses. Waists were high, to the top of a girl's ribs. The dresses were short, and girls sometimes wore light pants under them. Their dresses got longer as they got older. By the time they were teenagers, girls' dresses reached the floor.

Even diapers have changed. Long ago, baby bottoms were covered with grasses, moss, or animal skins. Then came cloth diapers that were fastened with safety pins. Urine leaked right through, so someone created a plastic covering to go over the cloth diaper. Today, we have disposable diapers that close with hook-and-loop strips and eco-friendly washable inserts that snap into reusable diaper covers.

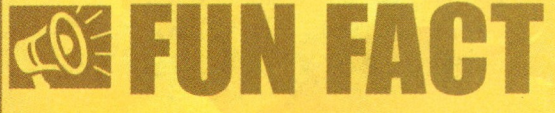

Imagine a world without sneakers! Athletic shoes were not invented until 1917. Before that, running shoes looked like slippers made of rubber and light canvas.

**Answer each question.**

1. Which is a reason from the text for a boys' celebration?

    A. They finally wore dresses.

    B. They finally wore pants.

    C. They finally wore sneakers.

2. Which was NOT true of girls' dresses?

    A. They had high waists.

    B. They were short until girls became teens.

    C. They were fastened with pins.

3. Which was NOT a baby diaper long ago?

    A. moss

    B. animal skins

    C. plastic bags

**Write two different meanings for each word from the passage.**

4. pants

_____

5. light

_____

**Plot each point. Connect the points in order to answer the question.**

1. (1, 1)
2. (1, 12)
3. (8, 12)
4. (8, 1)
5. (5, 1)
6. (5, 8)
7. (4, 8)
8. (4, 1)

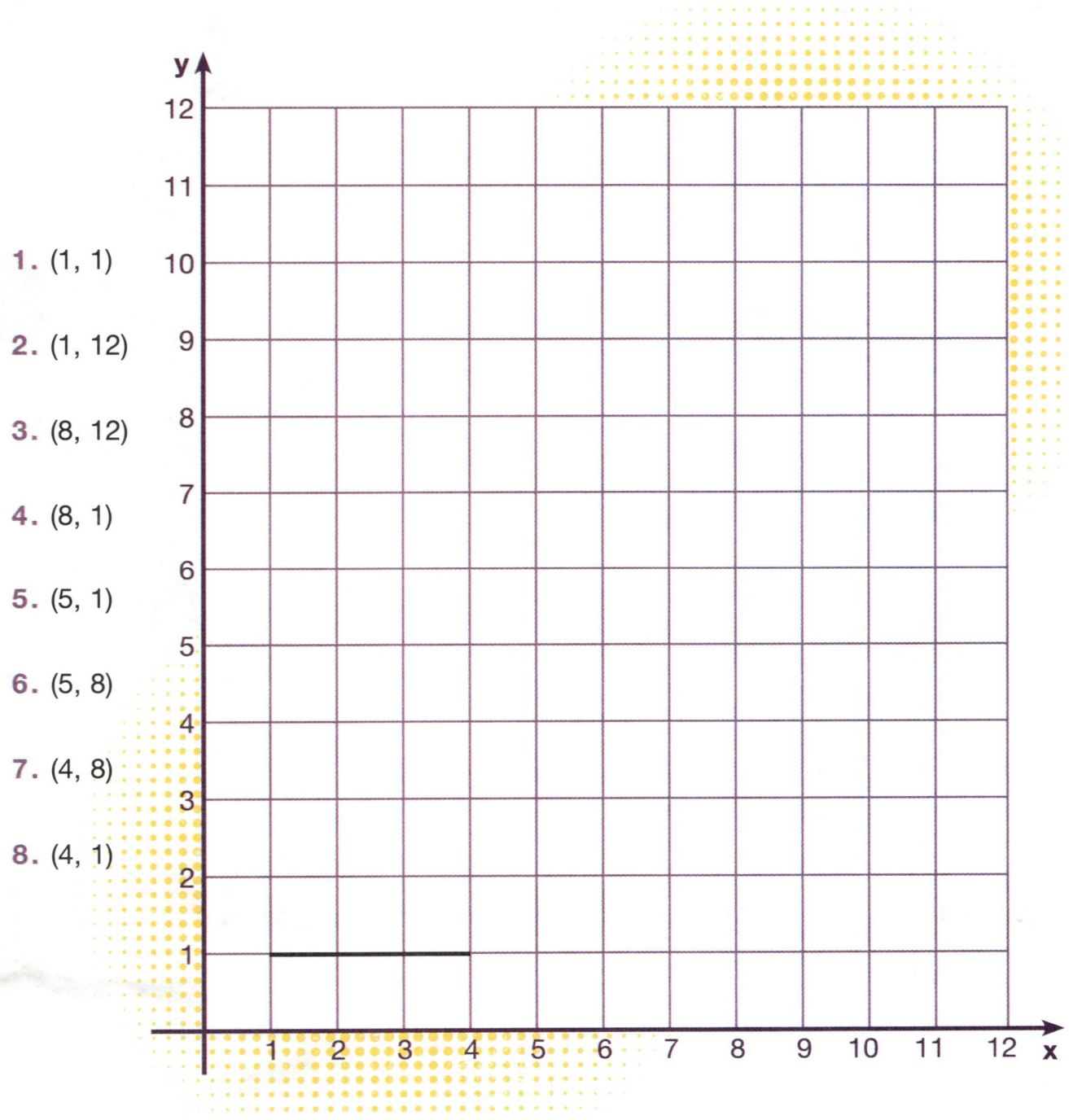

**Question**: What did you draw?

**Answer**: _____

**Follow the directions.**

Complete the synonyms for *pants*. Write the words in the puzzle.

**Down**

1. T__GH__S
2. B__OOM__ __S
3. __ __GG__ __GS
6. P__N__ALOO__ __ __
8. __REE__ __ES
9. T__OU__ERS

**Across**

4. __EA__S
5. KNI__ __ __E__S
7. SL__ __KS
8. BR__TC__E__
10. JO__ __ __ __RS

95

# MEDICAL REMEDIES

*BILE!? HARD PASS!*

Long ago, the cure was sometimes worse than the disease. Once, people swallowed elephant bile to treat bad breath. Snail slime was smeared on warts. Cuts were treated with moldy bread.

## FUN FACT

People would consume, through eating or drinking, various types of animal dung to cure what ailed them. Poo tea anyone?

Some ancient remedies almost made sense. Doctors used spider webs to bandage injured soldiers. Some scientists think the spider's strong silk strands are coated with something that fights bacteria. Doctors first poured honey and vinegar onto a wound, then covered it with spider web threads. This sounds gross, but it's way better than what was used centuries before.

Ancient remedies for a bad tooth included placing an insect cocoon against the tooth, chewing hot chilies, or spitting into the mouth of a frog under a full moon. To treat cataracts, medical textbooks might have suggested putting burned periwinkle flowers and honey in the eyes.

One especially odd cure for malaria called for the infected person to write the word *abracadabra* over and over on a piece of paper. Then, they would wear the paper around their neck for nine days. Hmmm…bet the fever would be gone by then anyway. Medical thinking has changed a lot over the centuries. Thank goodness!

**Write a response to each question.**

1. Write two or three sentences summarizing the text.

_____
_____
_____

2. What did the author mean by saying, "the cure was sometimes worse than the disease"?

_____
_____
_____

3. Which remedy intrigues you the most? Explain.

_____
_____
_____

**Find a synonym for each word from the text.**

4. strands _____

5. remedies _____

Use the table to solve each problem.

|           | Day 1   | Day 2   | Day 3   | Day 4   | Day 5   | Day 6   | Day 7  |
|-----------|---------|---------|---------|---------|---------|---------|--------|
| Patient A | 99.8°F  | 100.1°F | 100.8°F | 101.4°F | 102°F   | 102.1°F | 99.1°F |
| Patient B | 100.2°F | 101.4°F | 99.8°F  | 99.4°F  | 99.1°F  | 98.8°F  | 98.7°F |
| Patient C | 102.8°F | 102.4°F | 102.6°F | 102.1°F | 101.8°F | 100.5°F | 99.4°F |
| Patient D | 99.1°F  | 99.8°F  | 100.1°F | 101.4°F | 102.1°F | 101.7°F | 99.8°F |

Find the mean of each patient's temperatures over a week rounded to the nearest tenth. (Hint: To find the mean, add the temperatures and then, divide the total by 7 days.)

1. Patient A: _____

2. Patient B: _____

3. Patient C: _____

4. Patient D: _____

Find the median of each patient's temperatures over a week. (Hint: To find the median, or middle value, order the temperatures from least to greatest. Then, locate the one in the middle.)

5. Patient A: _____

6. Patient B: _____

7. Patient C: _____

8. Patient D: _____

# Follow the directions.

Use the letters to make words. Start with 2- and 3- letter words. Then, try to find a word that uses all the letters. (Hint: The word is a synonym of *remedy*.)

## C E E D I I M N

# BEAUTY SECRETS

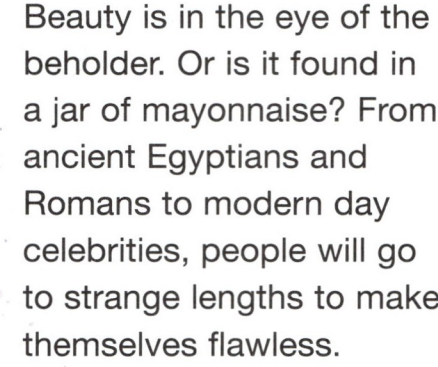

Beauty is in the eye of the beholder. Or is it found in a jar of mayonnaise? From ancient Egyptians and Romans to modern day celebrities, people will go to strange lengths to make themselves flawless.

Roman women had many beauty secrets. One special lotion to keep their faces creamy and soft was made with the sweat and dirt from sheep wool. Wealthy Roman women bought the sweat and dirt scraped off gladiators after a fight. These were used to make another popular face cream. Romans also applied face masks of crocodile dung, which they thought kept the skin healthy. Crocodile poo? No, thank you!

Both men and women of ancient Egypt enhanced their features with makeup. Ground ochre was used as lipstick. Kohl was used as eyeliner. And, burnt almonds were used to paint eyebrows and fill them in. Cleopatra, an Egyptian queen, is said to have taken baths in donkey milk. The lactic acid in milk exfoliated, or removed, dead skin cells. And honey was used to moisturize and disinfect the skin.

Today, some beauty-seekers may choose more conventional products. But, still, some celebrities are famous for their try-anything approach to beauty. Snake venom, snail slime, bird droppings, blood-sucking leeches, and even mayonnaise are just some of the unusual items used in famous celebrities' beauty routines. Maybe not much has changed since ancient times after all?

**FUN FACT** Need a pedicure? Try this beauty craze. Sit back and enjoy a relaxing spa session while sticking your feet in a container of skin-eating fish. Tickle, tickle, ouch!

**Answer each question.**

1. Another good title for the passage might be

    A. *Crocodiles Beware!*

    B. *Ancient Ways to Look Your Best*

    C. *How to Get Whiter Teeth*

2. Which was NOT used by the ancient Romans to look their best?

    A. crocodile dung

    B. gladiator sweat

    C. snail slime

3. In which liquid did Cleopatra bathe?

    A. donkey's milk

    B. olive oil

    C. honey

**Match each word to its definition.**

4. dung                                          feces or poo

5. conventional                                  remove surface of

6. exfoliate                                     common

**Solve for *n* in each problem.**

**1.** 14 + n = 24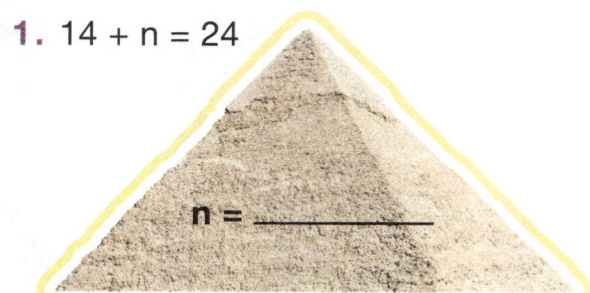

n = _____

**2.** n + 16 = 64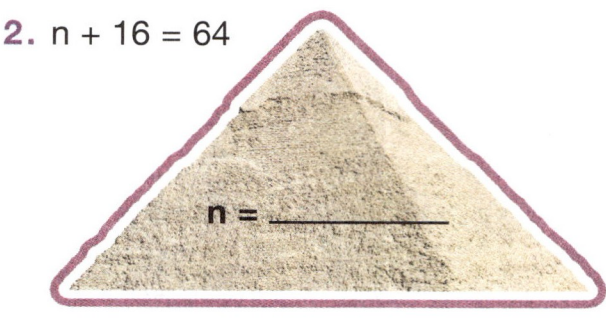

n = _____

**3.** 72 − n = 39

n = _____

**4.** 64 − n = 48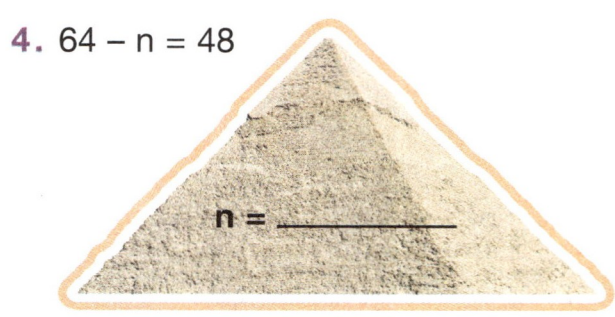

n = _____

**5.** 4 × n = 36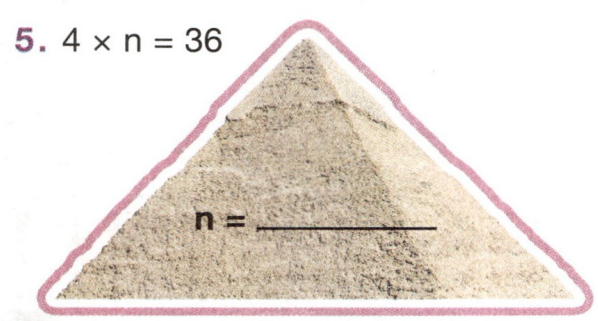

n = _____

**6.** n × 7 = 56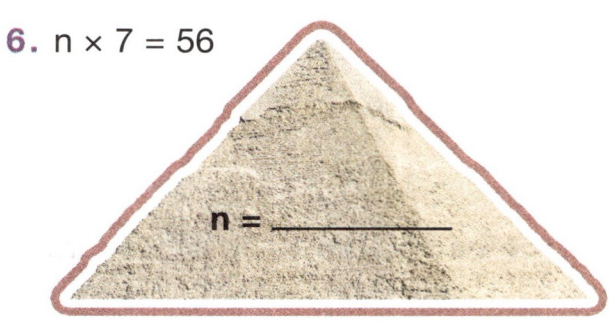

n = _____

**7.** 88 ÷ n = 8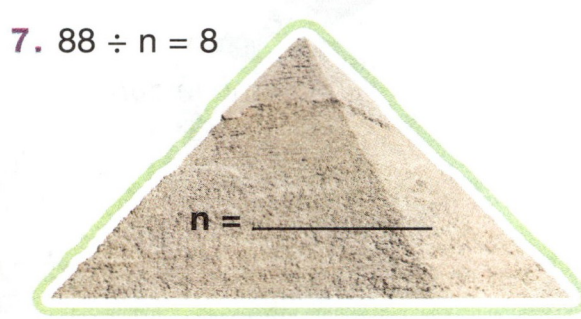

n = _____

**8.** 120 ÷ n = 10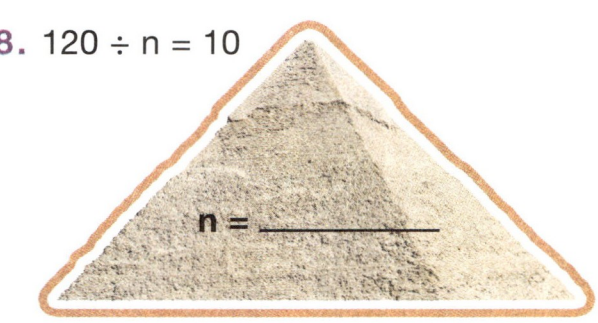

n = _____

# Follow the directions.

Find the area of each triangle. (Hint: Use the formula $\frac{1}{2} \times$ base $\times$ height.) Write the corresponding letters in order on the lines to answer the question.

**Question:** What kind of makeup do Egyptian mummies wear?

| 6 | 9 | 12 | 16 | 18 | 20 |
|---|---|----|----|----|----|
| M | S | R  | E  | C  | A  |

1. 3 in., 4 in.  _____ in.²

2. 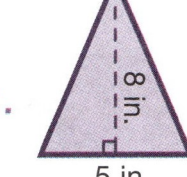 8 in., 5 in.  _____ in.²

3. 3 in., 6 in.  _____ in.²

4. 2 in., 9 in.  _____ in.²

5. 4 in., 9 in.  _____ in.²

6. 4 in., 10 in.  _____ in.²

7. 6 in., 4 in.  _____ in.²

8. 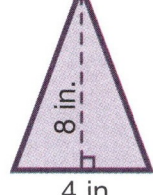 8 in., 4 in.  _____ in.²

9.  5 in., 8 in.  _____ in.²

**Answer:**

\_\_\_ \_\_\_ \_\_\_ \_\_\_ - \_\_\_ \_\_\_ \_\_\_ \_\_\_ - \_\_\_ \_\_\_

# HELP WANTED

What do you want to be when you grow up? A teacher? A doctor? How about a paper towel sniffer? Or a chewing gum taster? There are tons of extraordinary jobs out there just for you! Just use your senses!

Put your nose to work. Paper towel sniffers make sure towels are odorless before being packaged and sold to consumers. Or, you could be an armpit sniffer. People get paid to sniff armpits for companies who test the effectiveness of their deodorants. They need to know if they work, right? How about testing the effectiveness of chewing gum or mints? Be prepared to sniff some "bad breath" from strong scents such as garlic or coffee.

Food tasters have fun too. Companies such as Ben and Jerry's hire people to taste new ice cream flavors. Imagine tasting flavors like Chunky Monkey all day! A less exciting tasting job is pet-food taster. Pets can't speak for themselves, so you get to be their voice. Just pop some kibble in your mouth . . . and chew. Yes, you get paid for this.

If you are patient, you can become a line stander at ticket counters, sports events, store openings, or wherever crowds gather. Some people don't want to waste their time, so they hire a line stander to hold their place in line. Even more relaxing is the job of bed tester. That's when mattress companies or hotels pay you to take a nap. Zzzzz…

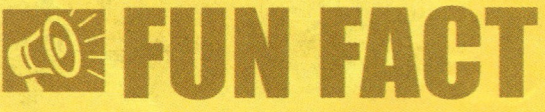

If you like to have fun and don't mind getting wet, you could be a water slide tester. They check water slides at amusement parks and carnivals to make sure they're safe and fun.

**Write T for *true* or F for *false*.**

_____ 1. People get paid to sniff toilet paper.

_____ 2. Armpit sniffers work for perfume companies.

_____ 3. You could get paid for taking a nap.

_____ 4. Food tasters always enjoy their jobs.

**Write a sentence for each word. Use the part of speech indicated.**

5. odor (n) _____

_____

6. slide (v) _____

_____

**Solve each row of problems.**

1. $\dfrac{1}{5} \times \dfrac{1}{2} =$ _____   $\dfrac{3}{4} \times \dfrac{1}{6} =$ _____   $\dfrac{1}{4} \times \dfrac{2}{6} =$ _____

2. $3 \times \dfrac{2}{5} =$ _____   $5 \times \dfrac{2}{3} =$ _____   $2 \times \dfrac{5}{7} =$ _____

3. $\dfrac{1}{5} \div 2 =$ _____   $\dfrac{1}{3} \div 4 =$ _____   $\dfrac{1}{2} \div 8 =$ _____

4. $4 \div \dfrac{1}{4} =$ _____   $5 \div \dfrac{1}{5} =$ _____   $12 \div \dfrac{2}{3} =$ _____

# Follow the directions.

You arrive at your new ice cream tasting job and find the front doors of the building locked. You check the other doors around the building too.

**Question**: How far do you walk around the building?

1 square = 1 m

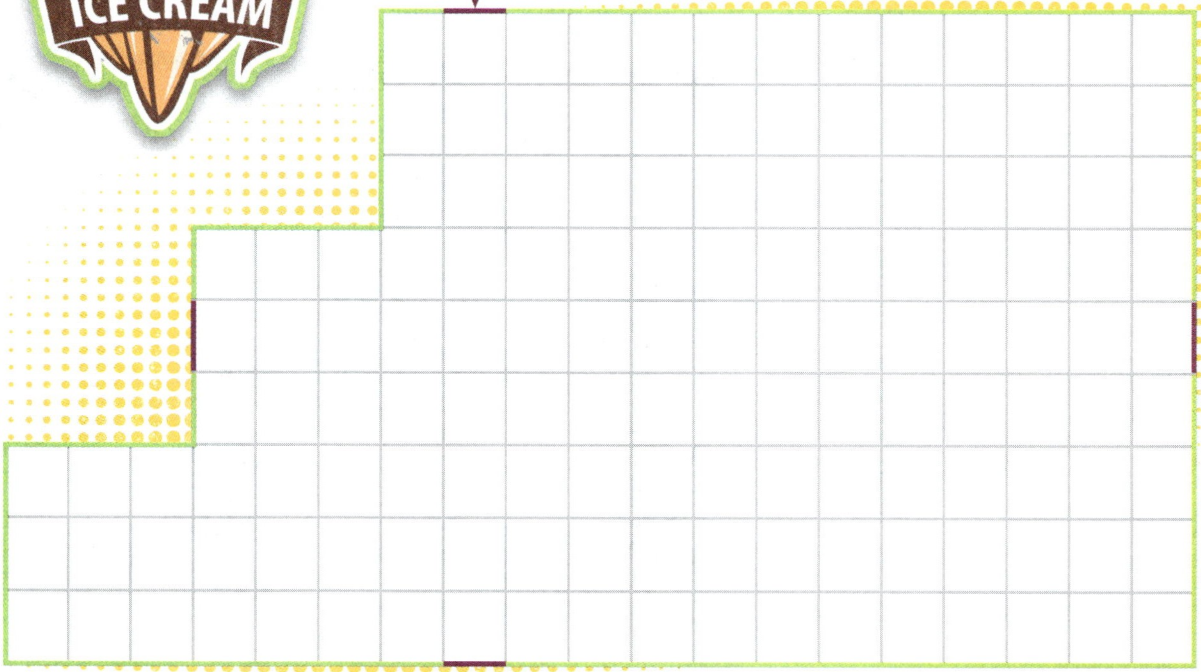

**Answer**: _____ meters

# MIRROR, MIRROR

Do you ever wish you had a twin brother or sister? Or, are you a twin or a multiple? Well, if you are a twin, take a good look at your sibling and observe the similarities and differences in your appearances.

Let's understand the different types of twins including a few rare types. The most common types of twins are fraternal and identical (monozygotic) twins. Fraternal twins are more like siblings. They share only 50% of their genetic material. Identical twins share 100% of their genetic material.

> GENETIC MATERIAL IS THE DNA YOU INHERIT FROM YOUR PARENTS. DNA DETERMINES YOUR APPEARANCE, HEALTH, PERSONALITY, INTELLIGENCE, AND SO MUCH MORE.

Mirror-image twins are one form of identical twins that scientists have started to study. These twins look the same but reversed. Features such as hair whorls or birthmarks appear on opposite sides of each twin. Mirror-image twins may have opposite handedness, gestures, and gaits.

Such small differences in twins are determined by the day in which the embryo splits. If an embryo splits too late, some unique differences develop. These can be as simple as a mole on the opposite side of the face or as complex as in rare cases, internal organs are reversed, which is called situs inversus.

MIRROR-IMAGE TWINS

 **FUN FACT** Although identical twins share DNA, there is one feature that is different—their fingerprints. DNA dictates a certain fingerprint appearance, but our movements in the womb affect how our fingerprints develop.

**Write a response to each question.**

1. What did you think the passage would be about when you read the title?

   _____

   _____

2. What is the difference between fraternal twins and identical twins?

   _____

   _____

3. Would you like to be a twin? Explain.

   _____

   _____

**Use context clues to explain the meaning of each word.**

4. feature

   _____

5. inherit

   _____

**Match each problem to its answer.**

1. 14 − 2 × 6 + 8 =

2. 25 − 11 − 8 × 1 =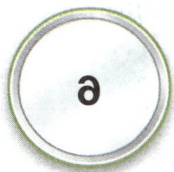

3. 4 + 2 + 5 × 4 + 1 =

4. 2 + 5 × 2 × 5 − 3 =

5. 9 × 9 − 1 × 5 =

6. 9 × 8 − 4 × 3 =

**Draw the mirror image of each figure. The first one has been done for you.**

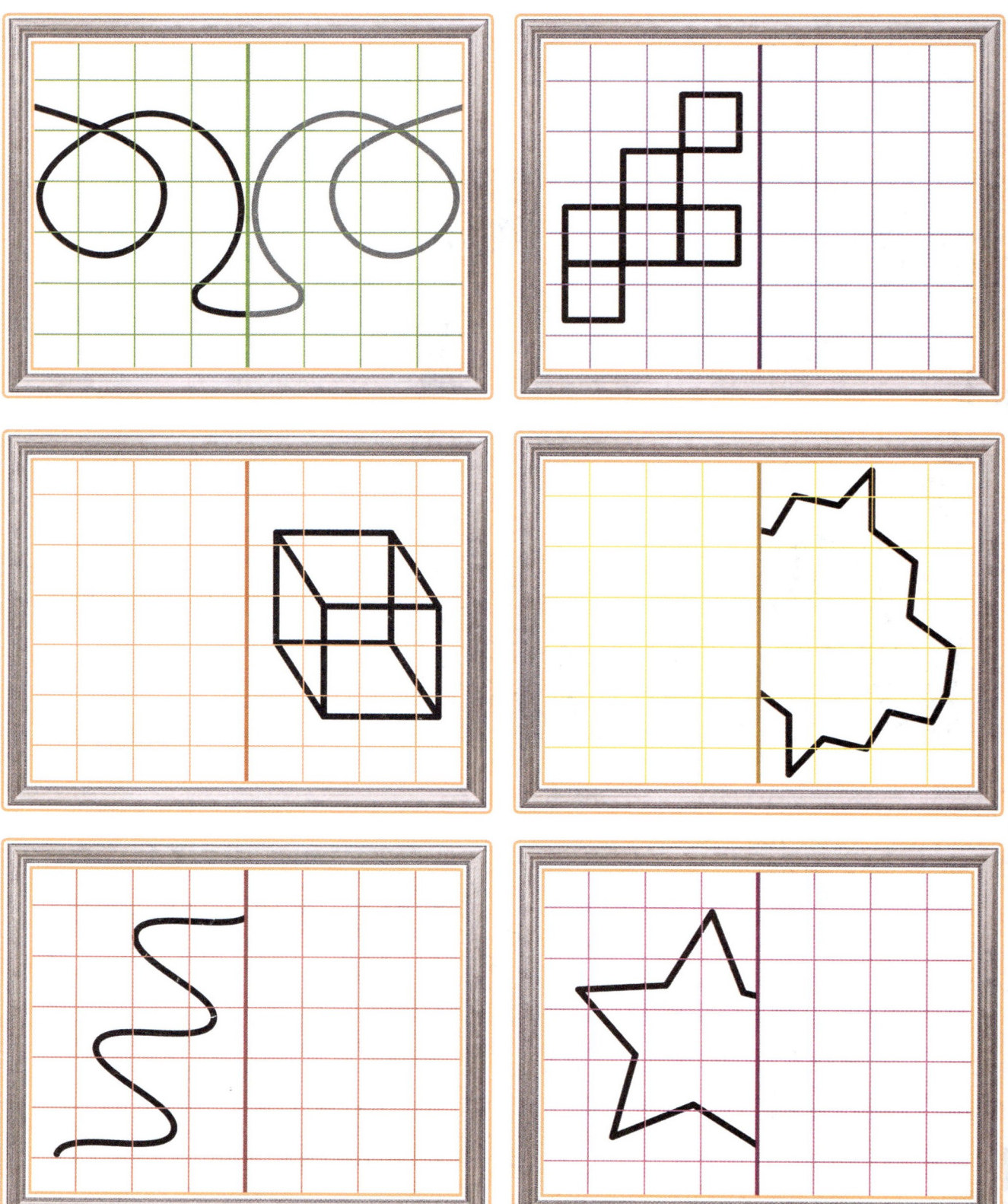

# HAIR WHERE!?

Have you ever seen a cat spit up a hairball? It's gross, right? Cats groom themselves by licking their fur. Fur is ingested in the process. But, guess what? People can also have hairballs.

CAT HAIRBALL

A human hairball is called a *trichobezoar*. Don't worry about trying to pronounce it unless you get one. It's just a fancy word for a wad of swallowed hair.

Human hairballs can be a serious problem if they are not vomited or passed. If large enough, they will get stuck in the stomach or intestine. When this happens, food cannot go down. It cannot go out either and will eventually be removed through surgery.

Relax. Everyone swallows a few of their own hairs from time to time. A stray hair is digested easily and passes through the digestive system without a problem. Humans shed between 50 and 100 hairs per day. One is destined for a plate near you!

## FUN FACT

A Cambridge-based hair stylist created a record-winning 225-pound (102-kg) ball of human hair. His kids begged him to make a hairball from all his clients' hair clippings. So, he did. And he named it, none other than, Hoss the Hairball!

## Answer each question.

1. What is the main idea of this passage?

    A. Cat hairballs are gross.

    B. Humans can get hairballs.

    C. Everyone swallows hair.

2. What is a human hairball called?

    A. trichobezoar

    B. foreign body bezoar

    C. lactobezoar

3. Which does NOT happen when humans get hairballs?

    A. They are removed by surgery.

    B. They are vomited up.

    C. They rot in the stomach.

## Write an antonym for each word.

4. fancy _____

5. serious _____

**Solve each problem.**

1. Hoss the Hairball weighed 97 pounds when the creator decided to donate it to a museum. He continually added to Hoss for 4 more years when it weighed 225 pounds. How many pounds on average did Hoss accumulate each year?

   _____ pounds

2. You decide to start building your own hairball using your dog's fur. If you brush your dog every day and get 0.25 pounds of hair each time, how many days would you have to brush your dog to get to Hoss's weight of 225 pounds?

   _____ days

**Write a response to the question.**

3. You also decide to get a cat and collect its hair each day which amounts to 0.2 ounces. Write an equation showing how many ounces or pounds of cat and dog hair you would collect in a year. Explain your solution.

   _____

   _____

   _____

**Follow the directions.**

To which plate will each hair lead? Trace the hairs to find out.

# WATCH WHAT I CAN DO!

A person with such flexible joints they can touch their palms together behind their back—pointing upward—may have Ehlers-Danlos syndrome (EDS). If so, their skin is extra stretchy too. They may bruise easily.

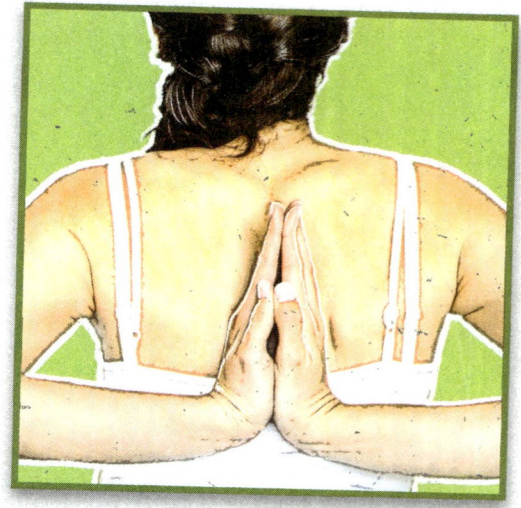

EDS doesn't keep most people from living a good life. In fact, some just work around it. Garry Turner has EDS. He can pull out the skin on his stomach more than 6 inches (15 cm). (Try it. Pinch your stomach skin and see how far out it comes.) Garry didn't let EDS get him down. He turned it into his superpower. In 1999, Garry showed off his special abilities in front of a live audience. He won the Guinness World Record for Stretchiest Skin.

You might think it would be cool to pull your cheeks way out or bend your thumb back to your arm, but people with EDS have to be careful. It's painful if their joints pop out of their sockets. Their skin pops back, but if injured, it doesn't heal well. When they need stitches, the stitches often tear out. There is no cure for Ehlers-Danlos syndrome. The good news is that scientists are working on it.

**FUN FACT** — Garry Turner probably has the stretchiest skin in the world. His skin stretches so far out he can pull his neck skin up over his chin to cover his mouth.

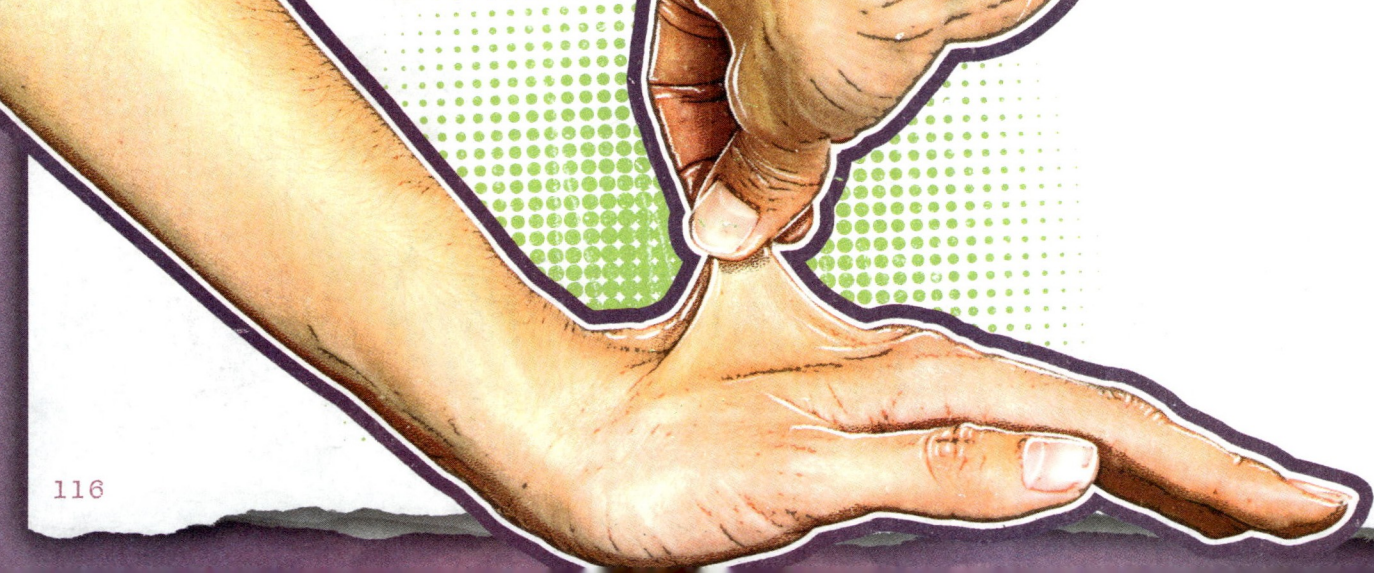

**Answer each question.**

1. What kind of figurative language is *stretchy skin syndrome*?

    A. personification

    B. alliteration

    C. metaphor

2. The word *flexible* does NOT mean

    A. easily changed.

    B. easily bent without breaking.

    C. unchangeable.

3. How did Garry Turner turn EDS into his superpower?

    A. He didn't let it bother him.

    B. He didn't try to hide it and won an award for it.

    C. He used his special abilities in private.

**Write an antonym for each word.**

4. upward _____

5. special _____

6. careful _____

**Write each number in expanded form.**

1. 45,689 _____

2. 172,405 _____

3. 373,013 _____

4. 1,049,620 _____

5. 2,830,501 _____

**Write each number in standard form.**

6. Fifty-six thousand four hundred two

   _____

7. One million three hundred twenty-seven thousand five

   _____

8. Seventy-eight thousand eight hundred forty-nine

   _____

9. Two million six hundred fifty-one thousand four hundred

   _____

10. One hundred sixty-three thousand seven hundred six

    _____

## Follow the directions.

Use the letters and numbers to determine each word's value. Then, answer the question.

| 1 | 2 | 3 | 4 | 5 | 6 | 7 | 8 | 9 | 10 | 11 | 12 | 13 |
|---|---|---|---|---|---|---|---|---|----|----|----|----|
| A | B | C | D | E | F | G | H | I | J  | K  | L  | M  |

| 14 | 15 | 16 | 17 | 18 | 19 | 20 | 21 | 22 | 23 | 24 | 25 | 26 |
|----|----|----|----|----|----|----|----|----|----|----|----|----|
| N  | O  | P  | Q  | R  | S  | T  | U  | V  | W  | X  | Y  | Z  |

F L E X I B L E = _____

S T R E T C H Y = _____

S Y N D R O M E = _____

**Question**: Which word has the largest value?

**Answer**: _____

# FOOT FAMILIES

Every foot is different, much like snowflakes. Even your left and right foot are not completely alike. Take off your shoes and compare those feet.

Some people believe you can tell a lot about your ancestry by the shape of your foot. This theory points out several different foot shapes—Roman, Greek, Egyptian, Germanic, and Celtic are just some examples. They believe that the angle of the toes reveal the region from which your ancestors originated.

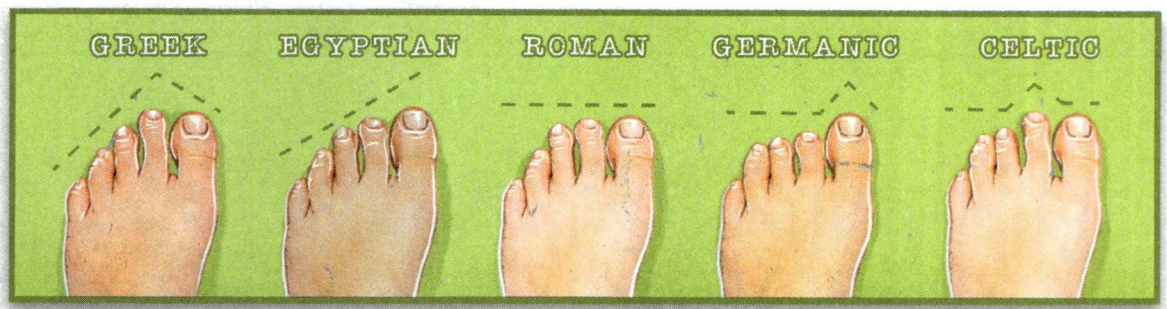

- The Greek second toe is longest, and the other toes descend from that one. (This is the most common foot shape in the world.)

- Egyptian toes line up from big to little, at a slant.

- The first three Roman toes are about the same length.

- Germanic feet have a larger big toe, and the others are the same length.

- Those with Celtic ancestry have an extra-long second toe.

Although entertaining to wonder, there is no scientific evidence backing this idea of ancestry. One has to wonder where the ideas may have come from, and why some ancestries are left out of the theories. Some say the ideas originated from looking at the feet of famous statues. What do you think? No matter the origin, foot shape can still be a fun dinner-table, well, under-the-dinner-table, topic.

 The average foot size has gone up two sizes in the last 70 years. This is because people have gotten taller, and they weigh more.

**Write T for *true* or F for *false*.**

_____ 1. Roman feet line up from big to little at a slant.

_____ 2. Celtic feet have an extra-long second toe.

_____ 3. The first three Egyptian toes are about the same length.

_____ 4. The Greek big toe is longer than the second toe.

_____ 5. The Germanic foot has a larger big toe.

**Write a sentence for each word. Use the part of speech indicated.**

6. ancestry (n) _____

_____

7. descend (v) _____

_____

**Write a response to the question.**

8. What do your feet look like? Draw and write about your foot and toe shape.

# Use the data to make a pie chart.

You take a survey of your 20 classmates' toe shapes. The results are below. Write the percentages for each shape.

| Toe Shape | Number of Classmates | Percentage of Class |
|---|---|---|
| Longer big toe | 5 | |
| Longer second toe | 9 | |
| All toes same length | 2 | |
| Other | 4 | |

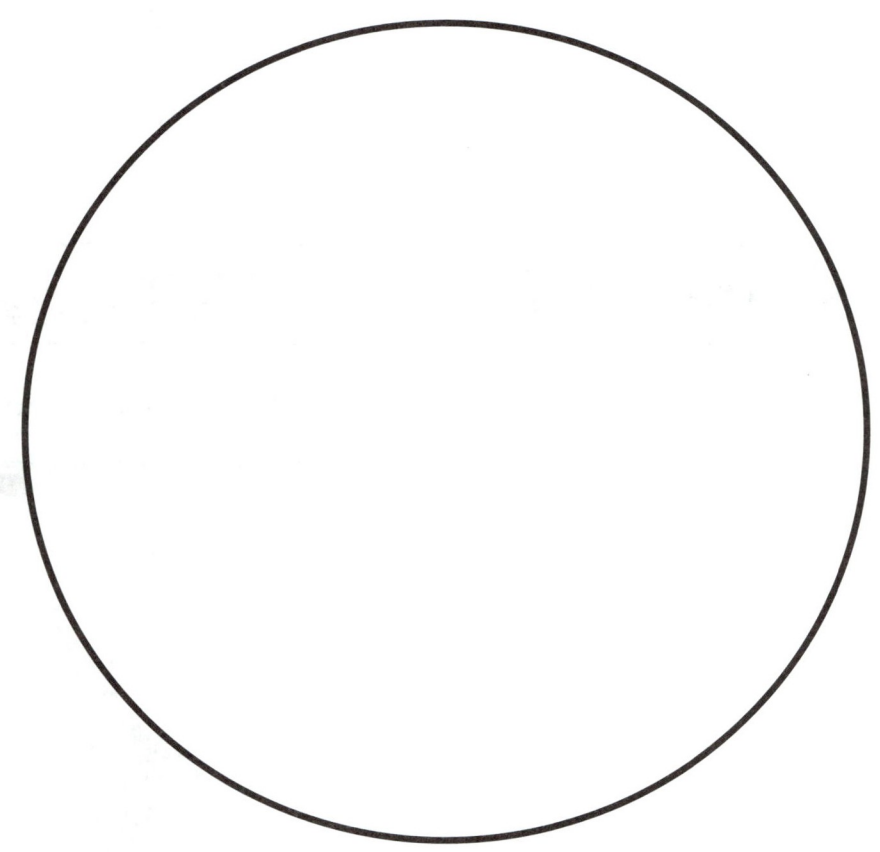

### Follow the directions.

A toy company wants to make a model of a foot statue that is smaller but exact. This is called a scale model. Look at the original statue's measurements and the length given for the model. What is the model's width?

**Statue**

2.2 m

6.6 m

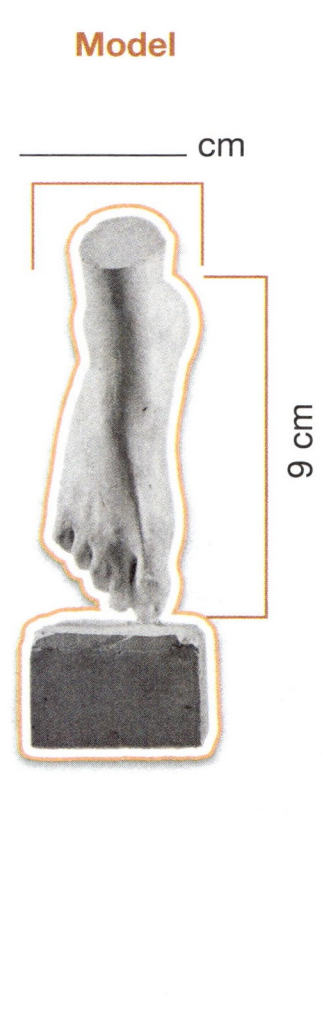

**Model**

_____ cm

9 cm

# WALKING IN CIRCLES

Our five senses help us every minute of every day. Our senses take in information and data that goes straight to our brains. Just like a computer, our brain then reads the data and reacts. It may tell you that you are hungry when you smell food cooking or contract a muscle to avoid a flame. When our bodies lose the ability to use one of our senses, our brains become confused reading signals and therefore have trouble performing certain tasks. How puzzling!

One such conundrum is why, when blindfolded, a person will walk in circles. And, sometimes, a person doesn't need to be blindfolded to walk in loopy paths. The movies show us examples all the time: lost people walking through the desert or a dense forest only to discover they've walked in a circle.

Scientists believe that the brain's balance-maintaining and body awareness systems work together to update the brain. Our brain uses visual clues and landmarks to help adjust our sense of "straight ahead." Little adjustments are made with every step to keep you on the right path.

THIS SEEMS FAMILIAR.

However, if your brain doesn't have these clues or other points of reference such as the sun, your brain won't make these adjustments. The normally small deviations from "straight" add up and the loopy walking begins.

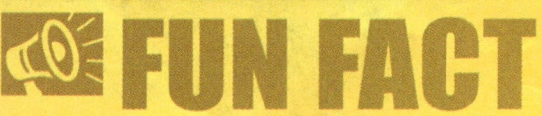

**FUN FACT** — Each person tends to veer to the right or to the left while walking. But this would only be troublesome if you are lost in a dense forest or desert.

### Write a response to each question.

1. Give an example of how you used one of your senses today. Explain.

   _____

   _____

2. What two systems work together to keep you walking on a straight path?

   _____

   _____

### Match each word to its definition.

3. sense                              to stray from a standard

4. conundrum                          a feeling

5. deviation                          a puzzling mystery or problem

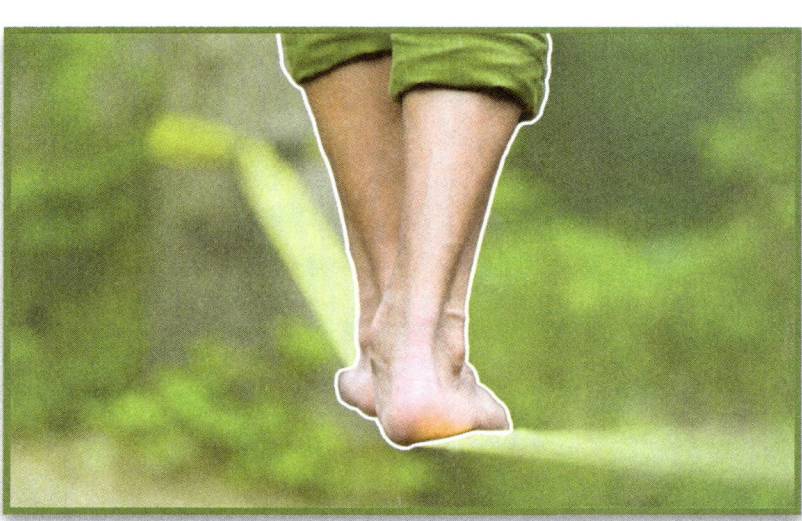

**Find the circumference of each circle to the nearest tenth.**

(Hint: Use the formula $C = \pi d$; $\pi$ is approximately 3.14 and $d$ is the diameter.)

1. 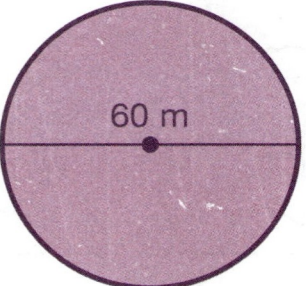   C = _____

2. 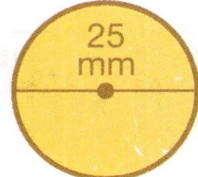   C = _____

3. 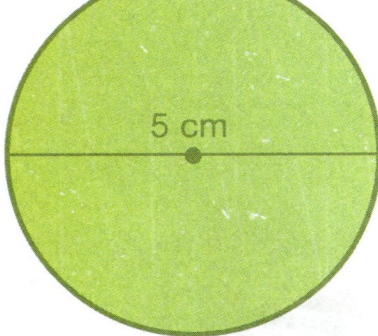   C = _____

4. 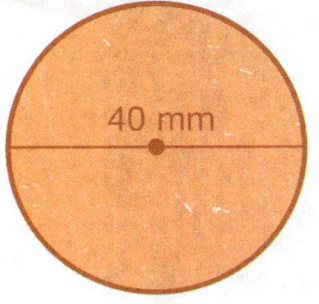   C = _____

# Follow the directions.

Find your way out of the forest. Then, answer the question.

**Question**: How many left-hand turns would you take to get out of the forest?

Answer: _____

# A RUSH OF BLUSH

Don't be embarrassed! It happens to all of us. Blood rushes to your cheeks and you can feel the heat. This is called blushing. No one knows exactly why it happens, but your brain recognizes a stress, good or bad, and goes into action.

Your brain notices when you feel excited, ashamed, or shy. It thinks you may be in trouble. It tells a gland to release adrenaline into your body. Adrenaline gives your body a boost in case there's trouble. Your breathing speeds up. Your eyes dilate. Your blood vessels expand so more blood and oxygen can reach body parts. That includes the skin of your face, which may feel warm to the touch. You are blushing.

Guess what! It's not only your face that's blushing. The blood also rushes to your stomach. When your face turns pink, so does the lining of your tummy. Yes, your tummy blushes too. But, take a deep breath. Once your body is calm and your blood circulation goes back to normal, the blushing will go away.

 Did you know that babies do not blush? Children do not blush until they're between 15 months and two years old.

**Complete each sentence with a word from the word bank.**

| adrenaline | dilate | embarrassed | expand | gland |

1. A _____ releases _____ when you feel shy or ashamed.

2. Your cheeks may blush when you feel _____.

3. Adrenaline causes your blood vessels to _____.

4. Your pupils _____ and open wider.

**Answer each question.**

5. According to the text, what happens to the stomach in times of stress?

    A. It can't digest food as well.

    B. Blood rushes there and turns the lining pink.

    C. The lining of the stomach starts to shrink.

6. Which is NOT a synonym for *expand*?

    A. enlarge

    B. widen

    C. shorten

I THINK THERE'S SOMETHING GOING ON IN HERE.

**Complete each sentence with number words.**

1. I am a quadrilateral with _____ pairs of parallel sides.

parallelogram

2. I am a quadrilateral with _____ pairs of parallel sides and _____ right angles.

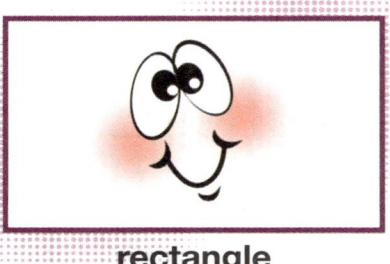
rectangle

3. I am a type of quadrilateral with _____ sides equal in length and _____ right angles.

square

4. I am a type of quadrilateral with _____ pairs of parallel sides and _____ sides equal in length.

rhombus

**Follow the directions.**

Let's play Blushing Squares!

**What you need:**

- 1 die
- red crayon

**How to play:**

Roll the die. Write the number rolled in both spaces of the first fact. Draw the square and make it BLUSH by coloring it red! Repeat. Try to fill the entire grid. An example has been done for you.

__3__ × __3__

_____ × _____

_____ × _____

_____ × _____

_____ × _____

_____ × _____

_____ × _____

_____ × _____

_____ × _____

_____ × _____

# VW SAUSAGES

When you think of Volkswagen, you might think of those cute little cars that look like bugs. Or, maybe you've seen some adventurers traveling in the retro-looking VW camping vans. Volkswagen, the company, makes cool cars, right?

PRODUCTION OF VW PART NO. 199 398 500 A

You may be surprised to learn Volkswagen produces more sausages than cars. Yes, sausages! Volkswagen vehicles are made in Germany, where spicy pork sausage links are more popular than cheeseburgers. In one year, Volkswagen sells more than seven million of its *currywurst* sausages.

It seems odd that a factory that makes cars also makes sausages. But, it's what's for lunch! Volkswagen makes sausages for their canteens. These canteens serve snacks and meals to VW employees on their lunch breaks. Sometimes the sausages are even given as a gift to a new customer. You'll also find the sausages sold at some supermarkets and football stadiums.

It's odd to find a car factory that makes sausages. The VW sausage even has its own part number, just like the brakes, the mirror, and the seatbelt. When you're hungry, just order *VW Part No. 199 398 500 A*. Do you want fries with that?

**FUN FACT** By the year 2025, VW will no longer serve meat of any kind. No more sausages! Instead, they think they can serve the planet better with vegan and vegetarian food.

**Write F for *fact* or O for *opinion*.**

_____ 1. Volkswagen makes cool cars.

_____ 2. Volkswagen makes more sausages than cars.

_____ 3. VW canteens serve meals to VW employees.

_____ 4. It's odd that a car factory also makes sausages.

**Write a synonym for each word.**

5. spicy _____

6. canteen _____

**Write a response to the question.**

7. What kind of vegan or vegetarian meal might VW serve in the future? Describe it and draw a picture.

**Solve each problem.**

1. Otto, Lina, and Hanna eat lunch together at work at the Volkswagen factory. Otto and Lina each eat 3 sausages a day, and Hanna eats 2. How many sausages do they eat altogether over 264 days?

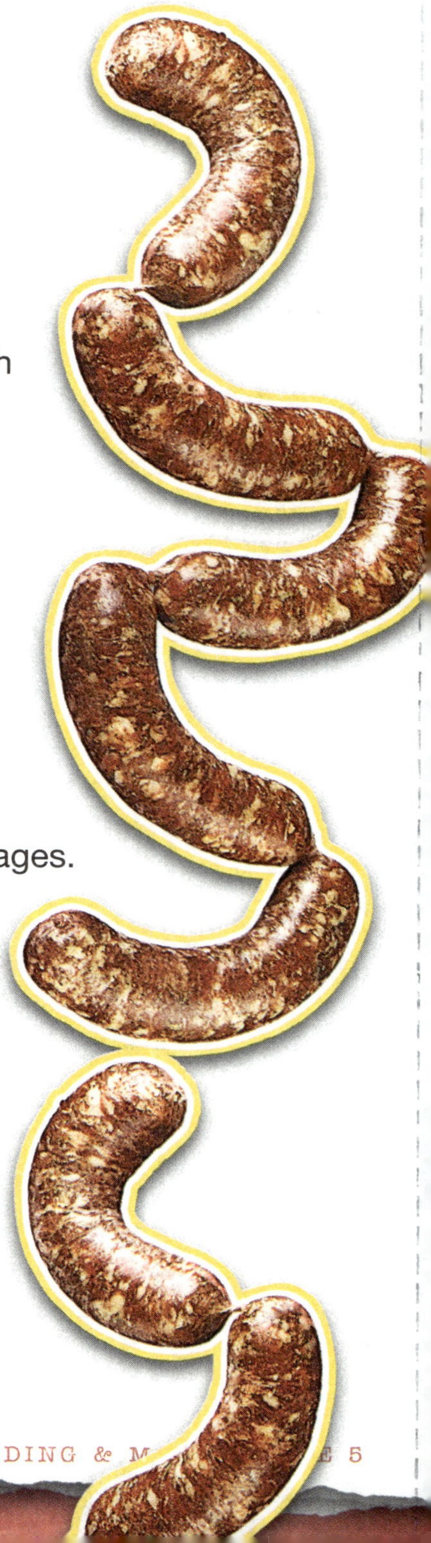

   _____ sausages

2. A Volkswagen dealership sells 15 cars for $23,000 each in one day. How much money do they make that day?

   $ _____

3. Over 28 days, the Volkswagen factory sells 5,488 sausages. How many sausages do they sell per day?

   _____ sausages

**Find the car parts in the word search below.**

AIRBAG  
BATTERY  
BRAKES  
ENGINE  
HEADLIGHTS  

HOOD  
HORN  
STEERING WHEEL  
TIRES  
TRANSMISSION  

```
S D F A G H T I R E S M N L O
M N B V I T H Y J K W H E Q P
I L X G H R P R E Z X E V B N
B R A K E S B K E O H A H Y T
D A C V B N Y A N W J D K M F
U V T N X Z J K G M N L V C G
E V B T N M Y N I U J I F D H
S C V B E T I B N S R G H G S
L Q W E R R T Y E U I H O O D
U I O P E D Y F G T G T H J K
C T J E V C M B Y T R S H P E
V H T R A N S M I S S I O N J
F S H J R Z D G J G R T R I O
D B I O Z X H B J G F C N N L
```

# UP PERISCOPE!

XBOX 360 CONTROLLER

PERISCOPE

Have you ever used an Xbox? It's a game console you hook up to a TV. People play games with it. Some even use the Xbox to watch movies. Sounds like fun! So, why is the US Navy buying them for their submarines? Don't Navy sailors have work to do?

The Navy is not telling its people to play video games when they should be working. They want to make it easier and cheaper to use submarine periscopes, those long, antenna-like tubes that zoom up and allow sailors to see above water. Many sailors had complained that the periscope joysticks were hard to use. They were also expensive, costing around $38,000 each.

The Navy found out they could use Xbox 360 controllers to operate the periscopes—for only about $20 each. And, if an Xbox controller breaks, they can simply find a nearby video game store on land to replace it. Now that's using common "cents."

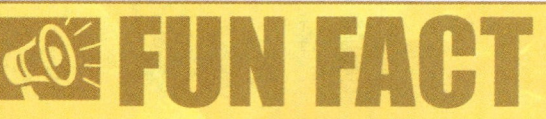

At the factory, an Xbox controller's buttons are pushed by a robotic hand over two million times to be sure they work and will last a long time.

**Complete each sentence with a word from the text.**

1. An Xbox is a game _____ you hook up to a TV.

2. An underwater submarine uses a _____ to see what is going on above water.

3. Xbox 360 _____ only cost about $20 each.

4. Periscopes today look more like _____.

**Write a response to the question.**

5. Sailors found a way to use an inexpensive item to perform a task instead of the expensive one. Write about a time when you were resourceful and found an inexpensive way to accomplish a task.

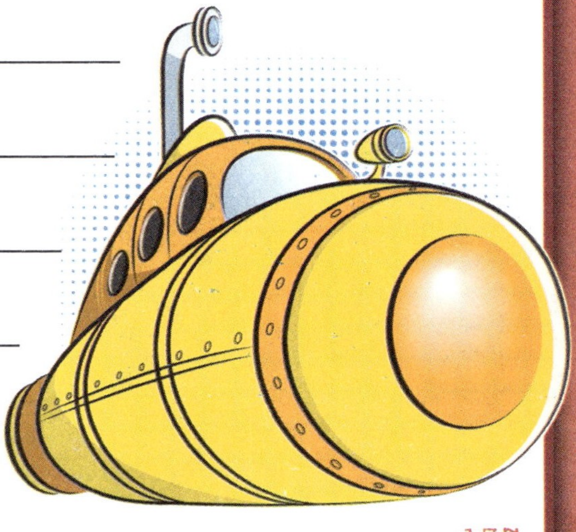

_____

_____

_____

_____

_____

_____

_____

_____

**Find the circumference of each circle on the submarines. (Hint: C = πd)**

1. C = _____
2. C = _____
3. C = _____
4. C = _____
5. C = _____
6. C = _____

# Follow the directions.

Use the code to reveal how another gaming device is used for important training.

| 1 | 2 | 3 | 4 | 5 | 6 | 7 | 8 | 9 | 10 | 11 | 12 | 13 |
|---|---|---|---|---|---|---|---|---|----|----|----|----|
| A | B | C | D | E | F | G | H | I | J  | K  | L  | M  |

| 14 | 15 | 16 | 17 | 18 | 19 | 20 | 21 | 22 | 23 | 24 | 25 | 26 |
|----|----|----|----|----|----|----|----|----|----|----|----|----|
| N  | O  | P  | Q  | R  | S  | T  | U  | V  | W  | X  | Y  | Z  |

__A__ __S__ __T__ __R__ __O__ __N__ __A__ __U__ __T__ __S__
 1   19   20   18   15   14    1   21   20   19

__U__ __S__ __E__   __V__ __I__ __R__ __T__ __U__ __A__ __L__
 21   19    5      22    9   18   20   21    1   12

__R__ __E__ __A__ __L__ __I__ __T__ __Y__
 18    5    1   12    9   20   25

__G__ __O__ __G__ __G__ __L__ __E__ __S__   __T__ __O__
  7   15    7    7   12    5   19     20   15

__T__ __R__ __A__ __I__ __N__   __F__ __O__ __R__
 20   18    1    9   14      6   15   18

__M__ __I__ __S__ __S__ __I__ __O__ __N__ __S__!
 13    9   19   19    9   15   14   19

# MAKE YOUR MARK

Punctuation is important. You would be horrified to read, "Let's eat Grandma." So, add a comma to say, "Let's eat, Grandma." You feel better. And, so does Grandma!

The first paragraph used 16 common punctuation marks. There are others you've probably never heard of.

| Mark | Description | Example |
|---|---|---|
| ‽ | The *interrobang* places the question and exclamation marks on top of each other for excited questions. | "What is that‽" |
| .~ | The *snark* mark works when you're being sarcastic. | Wow, beautiful weather we're having.~ (when it's dreary, stormy, and cold) |
| ♡? | When you're being nice, use the *love* point. It looks like a heart over a period. | I love my new puppy♡? |
| ⸮ | The *percontation* mark looks like a backwards question mark. This mark goes at the end of a rhetorical question. | Who knew⸮ |
| ⸮! | The *certitude* point looks like an exclamation point with a line through it. Use it when you are 100 percent certain. It communicates total decisiveness. | We're not going to the movies and that's FINAL⸮ |
| ?̷ | The *doubt* mark looks like a Z and a question mark together. Use it when you want to add skepticism. | Oh, you think you're going to the movies?̷ |

Punctuation has been around for more than 2,000 years. Early symbols were written into Greek plays to show the actors where to pause. And others used symbols to help with pronunciation.

### Add a punctuation mark to each sentence.

1. I adore you _____

2. You really didn't know _____

3. He bought what _____

4. Nice shoes, wish they fit _____

5. I said bedtime is at 8 p.m. and that's that _____

6. How could I be so careless _____

7. How could she _____

8. You think you're having six friends sleep over tonight _____

### Answer each question.

9. Which sentence is NOT a key detail from the passage?

    A. Punctuation is important.

    B. There are punctuation marks you've never heard of.

    C. There are 16 unfamiliar punctuation marks.

10. Why is using correct punctuation important?

    A. It makes sentences and paragraphs easier to understand for the reader.

    B. It helps the reader read faster and get done sooner.

    C. You can use fewer punctuation marks when you use the correct ones.

**Solve each problem.**

1. Freya got her language arts test back from her teacher. Out of 20 punctuation marks she had to add to a paragraph, she got 7 wrong. What percentage did she get wrong? What percentage did she get right?

_____ wrong    _____ right

2. In Landon's paper he used 54 commas, 60 periods, and 6 exclamation marks. Of the punctuation he used, what percentage was commas?

_____ commas

3. Serena took a survey of her class to see what their favorite unusual punctuation marks were. 12 answered interrobang, 10 answered love point, 9 answered snark mark, and 5 answered percontation mark. What percentage of her classmates answered snark mark?

_____ answered snark mark

**Follow the directions.**

Try your hand at using the unusual punctuation marks! Choose from one of the three writing prompts below. Write a response that includes at least three of the uncommon punctuation marks.

1. Imagine you found a map to a hidden passageway in your school. Write about your search and where it leads.

2. Imagine that you are invisible for one day. Write about where you go and what you do.

3. Imagine you are tasked with creating a new school rule. Write about the rule you created and what the first day was like with your new rule.

_____
_____
_____
_____
_____
_____
_____
_____
_____
_____
_____

# AN APPLE A DAY

Apples can be red, pink, yellow, and green. Did you know there are also black apples? Would you eat one?

Black Diamond apples are not truly black. Their skins are a deep purple—so dark they look black. Inside, the pulp is white and juicy. Black apples are grown in Tibet, an area of China. The orchards are found in a small city high in the mountains where the temperature changes a lot between day and night. They receive a lot of ultraviolet light from the sun. This is the reason for their bold color.

Black apples are sweeter than most and are in demand. These apples are much better for you! The supply is limited since the orchards are small and the apples must be carted down the steep mountainside. That's why they're so expensive and are only found in upscale stores two months out of the year. Some people are happy to pay as little as $7 to as much as $20 for just one black apple. They must be truly delicious!

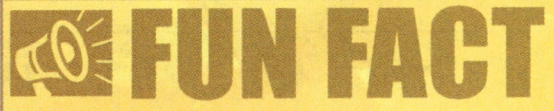 Another black apple is grown closer to home. The Arkansas Black apple is a tart apple grown in the American South.

**Write T for *True* or F for *False*.**

_____ 1. The temperature changes a lot between day and night.

_____ 2. Black apples are grown in the mountains of Tibet.

_____ 3. The apples are sold in discount stores.

_____ 4. The apples are carted down a steep mountain.

_____ 5. The apple pulp turns black.

**Answer each question.**

6. Which is NOT a reason for the Black Diamond apple's color?

   A. The apple is more expensive.

   B. The apples receive a lot of ultraviolet light.

   C. The temperature changes a lot between day and night.

7. What is the author's purpose for writing the text?

   A. to entertain you with tales about apples

   B. to inform you about black apples

   C. to persuade you to buy black apples

UNUSUALLY FUN READING & MATH GRADE 5

Answer each question.

1. Look at the chart of apples sold in a month. What is the probability that a person will buy each type of apple?

| Apples | Number Sold |
|--------|-------------|
| Black  | 10          |
| Red    | 42          |
| Yellow | 7           |
| Green  | 11          |

Black _____

Red _____

Yellow _____

Green _____

2. How would probability help a grocer keep the correct quantity of each apple in the store? Explain.

_____

_____

_____

**Follow the directions.**

Farmers can genetically modify, or change the DNA of, their crops. They do this to make their crops tolerate pests better, or even to make them taste better. Scientists have even made a pink pineapple! Imagine you were tasked with creating a new kind of apple and answer the questions.

1. What color would it be?

_____

2. What would it taste like? _____

3. What are the benefits of your new apple?

_____

_____

4. What kinds of recipes can your apple be used to make?

_____

_____

5. Draw and color your new apple.

# THANK THE MILITARY

McDonald's can't claim to have the very first drive-through window, but when they built theirs, they did it with heart. Their first window was built to help members of the military grab a burger. The service members from nearby Fort Huachuca, Arizona, wore uniforms most of the time. They were not allowed to appear in public in uniform, so they couldn't go to town for meals.

The local McDonald's noticed they didn't have customers from the base. Fort Huachuca was only two miles away. To feed their military fans, the restaurant put in a small window. An employee was assigned to take orders from the window so military members could stay in their cars. They couldn't come through the door, so McDonald's opened a window!

McDonald's solution was a success. In fact, the post commander and his daughter were the first in line when it opened! In less than 10 years, more than 5,000 McDonald's restaurants had drive-through windows. Today, you probably can't find a McDonald's without one.

## FUN FACT

French fries are the most popular menu item at McDonald's. They were on its very first menu. So if you want fries with that, just ask. But don't ask for their secret ingredient. They won't tell you.

**Answer each question.**

1. McDonald's first drive-through window was in

    A. New Mexico.

    B. Arizona.

    C. California.

2. Fort Huachuca is a

    A. military base.

    B. historical museum.

    C. war site.

3. Which did NOT happen as a result of the drive-through window installation?

    A. Military men and women were able to order burgers.

    B. The restaurant added fries to their menu.

    C. More than 5,000 McDonald's put in drive-through windows.

**Write two different meanings for each word from the passage.**

4. public

_____

_____

5. uniform

_____

_____

**Solve each problem.**

1. Miles orders lunch for his family. He orders a cheeseburger for $3.69, a chicken sandwich for $5.39, chicken nuggets for $5.29, a salad for $4.79, and 3 orders of fries for $2.69 each. How much does he spend in all?

    $ _____

2. Hudson spends $13.69 on lunch. Adalia spends $12.99. How much more does Hudson spend than Adalia?

    $ _____

3. Blake and Lucie go to lunch together. They get a soda for $1.29, juice for $2.69, a fish sandwich for $5.39, a double hamburger for $6.29, and 2 cookies for $2.09 each. They have a coupon for $5.99 off their order. How much do they spend?

    $ _____

Follow the directions.

Use the words in the word bank to solve the crossword puzzle clues about fun fast food facts.

| McDonald's    Wendy's    Burger King    Subway    KFC |
|---|

**ACROSS**

1. This sandwich shop was founded by a seventeen-year-old!

4. Fried chicken from this fast-food chain has become a popular Christmas meal in Japan.

5. Because of a popular meal that comes with a toy, this fast-food chain is the world's largest toy distributor.

**DOWN**

2. This fast-food royalty sold a hamburger with a black bun in Japan. Squid ink is what gave this burger its intense color!

3. This fast-food chain is the only one that sells baked potatoes.

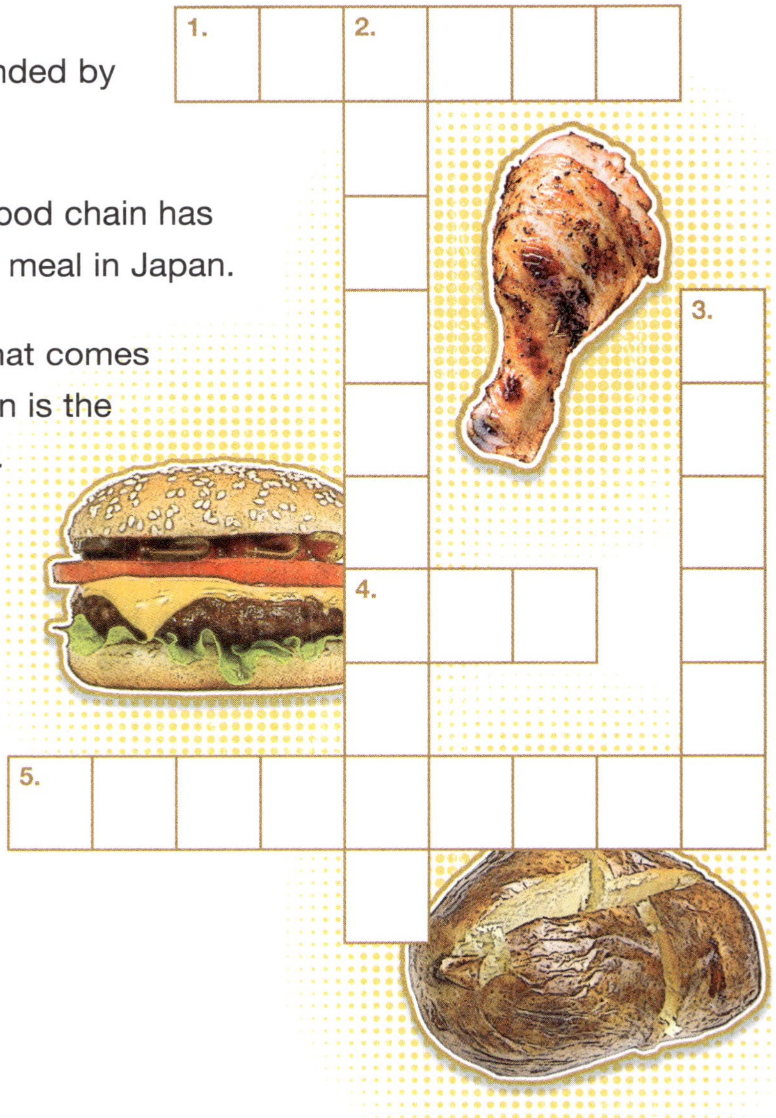

UNUSUALLY FUN READING & MATH GRADE 5      151

# DON'T BUG ME!

A word to anyone who enjoys painting nails, wearing lipstick, or using makeup—beware! There may be fish scales or crushed insect powder in them. A simple way to avoid any fishy products is to look at the label. If it says vegan and cruelty-free, you're in the clear!

FISH SCALES

PEAR CACTUS BUGS

Cleopatra, queen of Egypt, set makeup trends. Her favorite was a special shade of red lipstick. Oval-shaped bugs were picked off pear cactuses and processed to make the red coloring. The reds from these bugs are often used today in lipstick, nail polish, and even food. About 70,000 mashed bugs make one pound of this red powder. What a job for someone!

Do you like nail polish or lipstick that glitters? For a long time, the sparkles came from crushed fish scales. Check if there are fish scales in your makeup, shampoo, or shower gels. Do you see *Guanine* or *CI 75170* on the label? If so, it's got fishy parts. Another surprising ingredient in some makeup and soaps is algae, the aquatic plant. It is often used in soaps, shampoos, lotions, and creams. It is said to be great for hydrating your skin and hair. Next time you're around a pond, take a closer look at the green stuff floating on top. It might be an ingredient in your lotion!

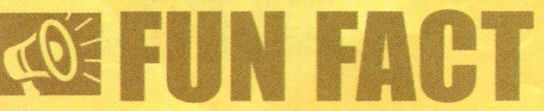

FUN FACT

The discovery of the special red color in the cactus bugs of the Americas changed the colors of European clothing. The dried bugs were shipped to Europe by the ton.

**Match each word to its definition.**

1. beware    item used to produce something

2. cactus    a desert plant

3. scales    tiny, thin plates that cover fish and some reptiles

4. ingredient    be very careful

**Write a response to each question.**

5. What do you think the author was implying when they said, "What a job for someone!"?

_____

_____

6. Write a better title for this passage. Explain why it is better.

_____

_____

_____

_____

Use the graph to answer each question.

1. List the nail polish colors from most liked to least liked.

   _____

2. What fraction of people like purple nail polish the best? _____

3. How many more people like pink than blue? _____ people

# Follow the directions.

Help Cleopatra find the red bugs for her beauty products! Write the letters you pass in order on the lines to finish the fact.

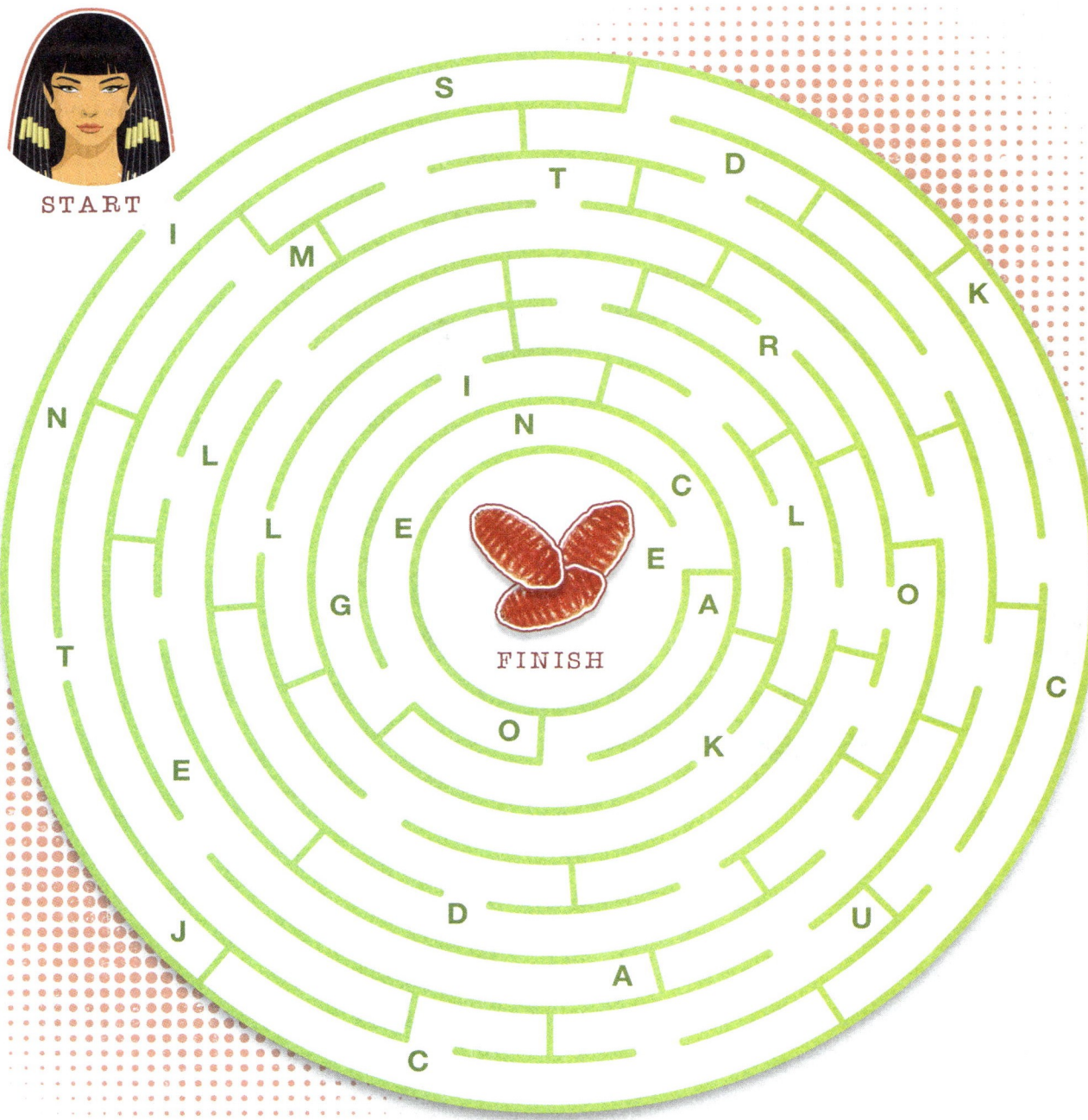

While history remembers her for her beauty, Cleopatra's biggest strength was her

____ ____ ____ ____ ____ ____ ____ ____ ____ .

# WHAT'S FOR DINNER?

Canada is famous for great things such as ice hockey, maple syrup, the Northern Lights, and good manners. What else do you know about Canada? Did you know they eat more macaroni and cheese than any other country?

This cheesy, oozy, comfort food is popular all around the world. About a million blue and yellow boxes of everyone's favorite mac 'n' cheese fly off store shelves every day. Do the math. That's seven million boxes a week!

But, no country buys more mac 'n' cheese than Canada. They take home 1.7 million of the seven million boxes sold weekly around the globe. That comes out to about three boxes for each Canadian. That's a lot of mac 'n' cheese. This yummy, cheesy pasta is the top-selling grocery item in Canadian shopping carts. Some people think this is because of Canada's long, cold winters. Nothing like a big bowl of cheesy macaroni to warm you up, eh?

Even a former Canadian prime minister, Paul Martin, confessed that mac 'n' cheese was his favorite food. Another prime minister, Stephen Harper, cooked it for his kids but added hot dogs.

**Write F for *fact* or O for *opinion*.**

_____ 1. No country eats more mac 'n' cheese than Canada.

_____ 2. That's a lot of mac 'n' cheese.

_____ 3. Mac 'n' cheese is a yummy, cheesy pasta.

_____ 4. Canadians buy 1.7 million boxes of mac 'n' cheese a week.

**Write a response to each question.**

5. Why did the author call macaroni and cheese a "comfort food"?

_____

_____

6. What is your favorite comfort food?

_____

_____

**Solve each problem.**

1. Jace cooks lunch for his family. His sister eats $\frac{2}{7}$ of the macaroni and cheese. His brother eats $\frac{5}{14}$. What fraction is left for Jace?

   _____

2. Nadia is taking a poll to see what the favorite food in her class is. Of the class, $\frac{2}{9}$ say their favorite food is peanut butter and jelly sandwiches, $\frac{9}{27}$ say their favorite food is pizza, and the rest say their favorite food is macaroni and cheese. What percentage of the class likes macaroni and cheese best?

   _____

3. On Monday, a grocery store sells $\frac{8}{36}$ of its macaroni and cheese supply. On Tuesday, the store sells $\frac{5}{18}$ of its supply. How much of the macaroni and cheese supply is left?

   _____

# Follow the directions.

Mac 'n' cheese may be a favorite of Canada, but what foods are eaten most around the world? Find the names of the most popular foods in the puzzle.

WHEAT
CHICKEN
CORN
EGGS
RICE

PORK
SORGHUM
POTATOES
CASSAVA
BEEF

```
A B C S C G D R O M D S E L R
O M D H P O T A T O E S K O I
I T G R N C R N O R S D T N C
O B V C F B N N H F D Q A I E
I E B J T Y U I O N J P W L K
D E Z X C V B A M S D F H G H
E F Q W E C R U T Y H I E I O
V C X Z M N H D F G H J A Y U
E B N M O G L I Y T E W T M N
T G F G R L Y T C F M P I C V
W E G O T Y U N B K J D O N A
C A S S A V A S F G E P I R L
Q W E R T Y U I O P H N D H K
```

UNUSUALLY FUN READING & MATH GRADE 5

159

# SAY WHAT?

Have you ever wanted to explain something, but there wasn't a word for it? Not everything is covered in the English language. Maybe there's a word in another language.

What do you call a joke so bad it makes you laugh? Indonesia's slang for that is *jayus*. We also laugh at people who sing made-up words when they don't know the lyrics. In France, that's called *chanter en yaourt*. Oddly, that means "yogurt singing." If they're singing at your birthday party, you're the *feestvarken*, Dutch for "party pig." If you accidentally overeat in the country of Georgia, it's *shemomechama*. And if you're eating because you're sad, the Germans have the perfect word for you. *Kummerspeck* is German slang for emotional eating or "grief bacon."

Some foreign words do not translate well. In Portuguese, *dedos do pe* translates to "foot fingers," but the word really means toes. In Afrikaans, *papier vampier* translates to "paper vampire," but it is the word for stapler. And *toiletbril* in Dutch translates to "toilet glasses." In fact, it means toilet seat.

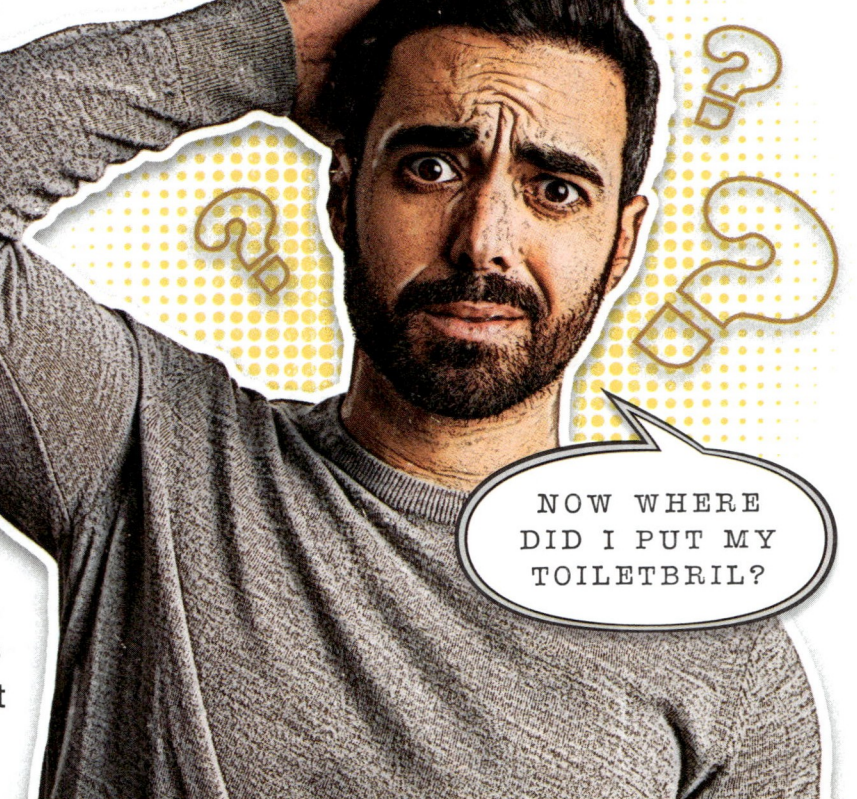

NOW WHERE DID I PUT MY TOILETBRIL?

**FUN FACT** Have you ever pretended no one is home when someone knocked on your door? What's that called? In Japan, they call it *irusu*.

**Match each foreign word or phrase to its English translation.**

1. *irusu* — paper vampire

2. *jayus* — party pig

3. *feestvarken* — foot fingers

4. *dedos do pe* — pretending no one's home

5. *papier vampier* — laughing at a bad joke

**Write a response to each question.**

6. Write a sentence using the word *language*. Use it as a noun.
_____
_____

7. What foreign word or phrase do you find most interesting? Explain.
_____
_____

**Solve each problem.**

1. Zoe and Ethan could use the word *shemomechama* right about now! They ate too many cookies and are feeling stuffed. Zoe ate $5\frac{3}{4}$. Ethan ate $4\frac{1}{4}$. How many more cookies did Zoe eat than Ethan?

_____ cookies

2. Declan sings in his school choir. They have a concert coming up. Declan has to learn the words to the songs so he doesn't do any *chanter en yaourt*. On Monday, he learns $3\frac{3}{8}$ songs. On Tuesday, he learns $2\frac{4}{8}$ songs. How many songs did he learn altogether?

_____ songs

3. Cora is the *feestvarken* and throws a pizza party for her birthday. She orders $6\frac{1}{2}$ cheese pizzas and $3\frac{1}{2}$ veggie pizzas. $7\frac{1}{2}$ pizzas get eaten. How many pizzas were left?

_____ pizzas

# Follow the directions.

Use the code to reveal another word we don't have in English and its definition.

| 1 | 2 | 3 | 4 | 5 | 6 | 7 | 8 | 9 | 10 | 11 | 12 | 13 |
|---|---|---|---|---|---|---|---|---|---|---|---|---|
| A | B | C | D | E | F | G | H | I | J | K | L | M |

| 14 | 15 | 16 | 17 | 18 | 19 | 20 | 21 | 22 | 23 | 24 | 25 | 26 |
|---|---|---|---|---|---|---|---|---|---|---|---|---|
| N | O | P | Q | R | S | T | U | V | W | X | Y | Z |

"__ __ __ __ __" is a __ __ __ __ __ __ word used
   8  25  7  7  5            4  1  14  9  19  8

to describe __ __ __ __ __ __ __
             1  19  5  14  19  5  15  6

__ __ __ __ __ __ __,
 3  15  26  9  14  5  19  19

__ __ __ __ __ __ __ __, and
 8  1  16  16  9  14  5  19  19

__ __ __ __ __ __ __, especially when
 3  15  13  6  15  18  20

__ __ __ __ __ __ __ __ __ __ __
 1  18  15  21  14  4     12  15  22  5  4

__ __ __ __.
15  14  5  19

# A BETTER MOUSETRAP

Mice can be pests, and dangerous pests at that. People have tried for centuries to build a good mousetrap. They wanted to stop these pesky critters from eating their food and spreading disease. Today, the Patent Office has issued more than 4,440 mousetrap patents. But some traps are much better than others.

In 1861, a company named Colin Pullinger & Son's invented a trap that was a real game changer. They called it the *Perpetual Mouse Trap*, saying it should last forever. The sturdy box had an opening in the middle. Inside was a kind of seesaw. Once the trap was baited, a mouse would jump in. Once inside, the seesaw would teeter and the mouse would fall to one side. Once the mouse drops, it's trapped inside, still alive.

A museum in England has a Perpetual Mouse Trap on display. In 2016, a museum staff member found a mouse in it. The trap had no bait and at 155 years old still worked perfectly! As Colin Pullinger & Son's said, their mousetraps "last a lifetime." One of the museum staff said it best, "Let's pay tribute to the Victorians, and how wonderfully they managed to make things."

## FUN FACT

Cartoons often show mice eating cheese. The best bait to use is peanut butter. However, mice also will stop to snack on chocolate, meat, or wet cat food.

**Follow the directions.**

Number the sentences from 1 to 5 to show the order of events in the passage.

_____ 1. In 1861, Colin Pullinger & Son's invented the Perpetual Mouse Trap.

_____ 2. The Patent Office has issued more than 4,440 mousetrap patents.

_____ 3. In 2016, a mouse was caught in the Perpetual Mouse Trap!

_____ 4. People have tried for centuries to build a good mousetrap.

_____ 5. A museum in England has a Perpetual Mouse Trap on display.

**Answer each question.**

6. Which is NOT a good definition of the word *pest*?

    A. delight

    B. annoyance

    C. irritant

7. What does the word *perpetual* mean in the name of the Colin Pullinger & Son's mousetrap?

    A. quick

    B. temporary

    C. forever

**Find the perimeter and area of each mousetrap.**

1.

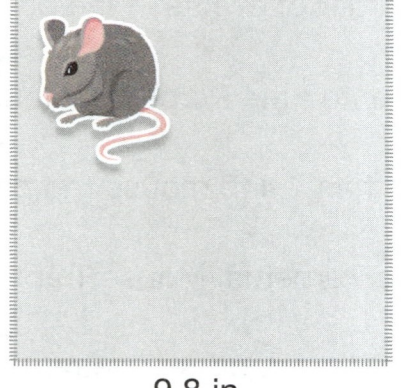

9.8 in.

9.8 in.

Perimeter _____

Area _____

2.

8.3 cm

20.2 cm

Perimeter _____

Area _____

3.

12.4 in.

15.7 in.

Perimeter _____

Area _____

4.

16.5 cm

11.9 cm

Perimeter _____

Area _____

# Follow the directions.

Help this mouse find what it REALLY wants to eat! Draw a path through the factors of 108.

# BITTY BOTS

The smallest-ever remote-controlled robot was built in the shape of the peekytoe crab, a Maine shellfish. The robot is about half a millimeter wide. That's really tiny, just half the size of a sharp pencil point. It is way smaller than a flea!

This mini, robotic crab is made of special materials. Although simply built, it can walk, jump, twist, bend, crawl, and turn on command. It can even crawl sideways, just like a live crab. However, it cannot do anything on its own. Its movements are controlled from a distance by a laser. The laser warms different parts of the little robot, making it move this way and that. It is not fast but can move half an inch (1 cm) in about 30 seconds.

ENLARGEMENT OF A ROBOTIC CRAB

Scientists imagine these tiny robots will be able to work in spaces too small for human hands. This includes squeezing into engine parts and repairing them or crawling into human bodies to stop bleeding or other lifesaving tasks.

## FUN FACT

Scientists are also working on other tiny robots. These look more like beetles, crickets, and inchworms. The goal is to get these little robots to do jobs humans are too big to do.

**Answer each question.**

1. How is the text organized?

    A. compare and contrast

    B. sequence

    C. description

    D. cause and effect

2. According to the text, why are tiny crab robots getting so much attention?

    A. They can perform lifesaving tasks in human bodies.

    B. They can repair small engine parts.

    C. They can do jobs that big human hands cannot do.

    D. All of the above

**Write a synonym from the text for each word.**

3. stroll

    _____

4. order

    _____

5. fixing

    _____

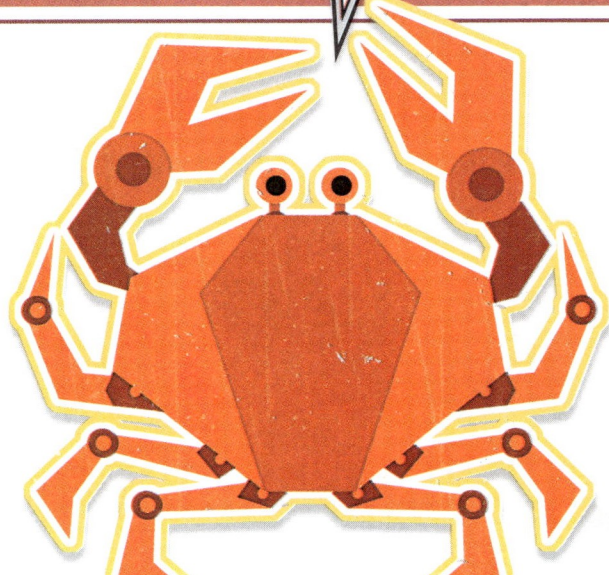

A LITTLE TO THE LEFT...

**Use >, <, or = to compare the distances of the laser beams.**

1. 10 inches _____ 10 centimeters

2. 2 kilometers _____ 2 miles

3. 1 meter _____ 100 centimeters

4. 14 inches _____ 3 feet

5. 2 meters _____ 1 yard

6. 1 yard _____ 100 centimeters

**Follow the directions.**

Each robot is good at one skill. No two robots have the same skill. Use the clues to figure out each robot's strength. Color the correct box for each robot and skill.

- The green robot can't clean or build.

- The orange robot can get you from one place to another.

- The yellow robot can't drive or cook.

- The red robot can't stand a messy room.

- The blue robot knows its way around a kitchen.

|  | Driving | Cleaning | Building | Cooking | Dancing |
|---|---|---|---|---|---|
| Red |  |  |  |  |  |
| Orange |  |  |  |  |  |
| Yellow |  |  |  |  |  |
| Green |  |  |  |  |  |
| Blue |  |  |  |  |  |

# FOOD FADS

Food fads come and go. We still eat some of the foods your grandparents ate in the 1960s and '70s. Other popular recipes vanished into thin air. Let's not talk about pickled tongue or pigs' feet. And how about that tuna-berry sandwich? Think tuna on bread covered with cream of chicken soup. No berries!

Molded Jell-O salads were all the rage, loaded with nuts, celery, carrot shreds, pineapple tidbits, and 7-Up—topped with whipped cream for dessert. Jell-O, avocado, and tuna chunks made a delicious side salad. These paired perfectly with meatloaf. Meatloaf was inexpensive and easy to make by mixing onions, eggs, and breadcrumbs with hamburger. Adventurous cooks added in bananas, peaches, or a layer of green beans.

GELATIN SALAD WITH FRUIT

Casseroles were crowd pleasers. The Wieneroni Casserole combined hot dogs, syrup, and pasta in one bowl. Fill a pie crust with hamburger meat and cover it with cheese and ketchup to make Cheeseburger Pie. Bologna Biscuits with Vegetables combined bologna, carrots, green beans, and tomatoes. Drop a plop of biscuit dough on top and bake. Some people even made bologna cakes, layering bologna slices with ranch dressing and cream cheese. Are you hungry yet?

**FUN FACT**

*Spam*, invented in 1937, is a portmanteau word for spiced ham. The canned meat is still sold in stores today. Spam fries quickly. Smear jam on it, add a clump of mashed potatoes, and you have a "Piggy Back."

**Write a response to each question.**

1. Choose two foods from the text you would eat. Explain.

   _____

   _____

2. Choose two foods from the text you would not eat. Explain.

   _____

   _____

**Match each idiom to its meaning.**

3. all the rage                                              mysteriously

4. into thin air                                              popular

5. crowd-pleaser                                       the latest fashion

PICKLED PIGS' FEET

**Follow the directions.**

Kaden is throwing a '70s-themed party at his apartment. He wants to have decorations, music, food, and costumes to get his guests in the groove. Plot the locations on the grid. Connect the locations to show a path he will take around the neighborhood. Start and end at his apartment.

Apartment (2, B)            Party Store (7, H)

Bank (4, G)                 Record Store (5, D)

Market (11, E)              Thrift Shop (8, C)

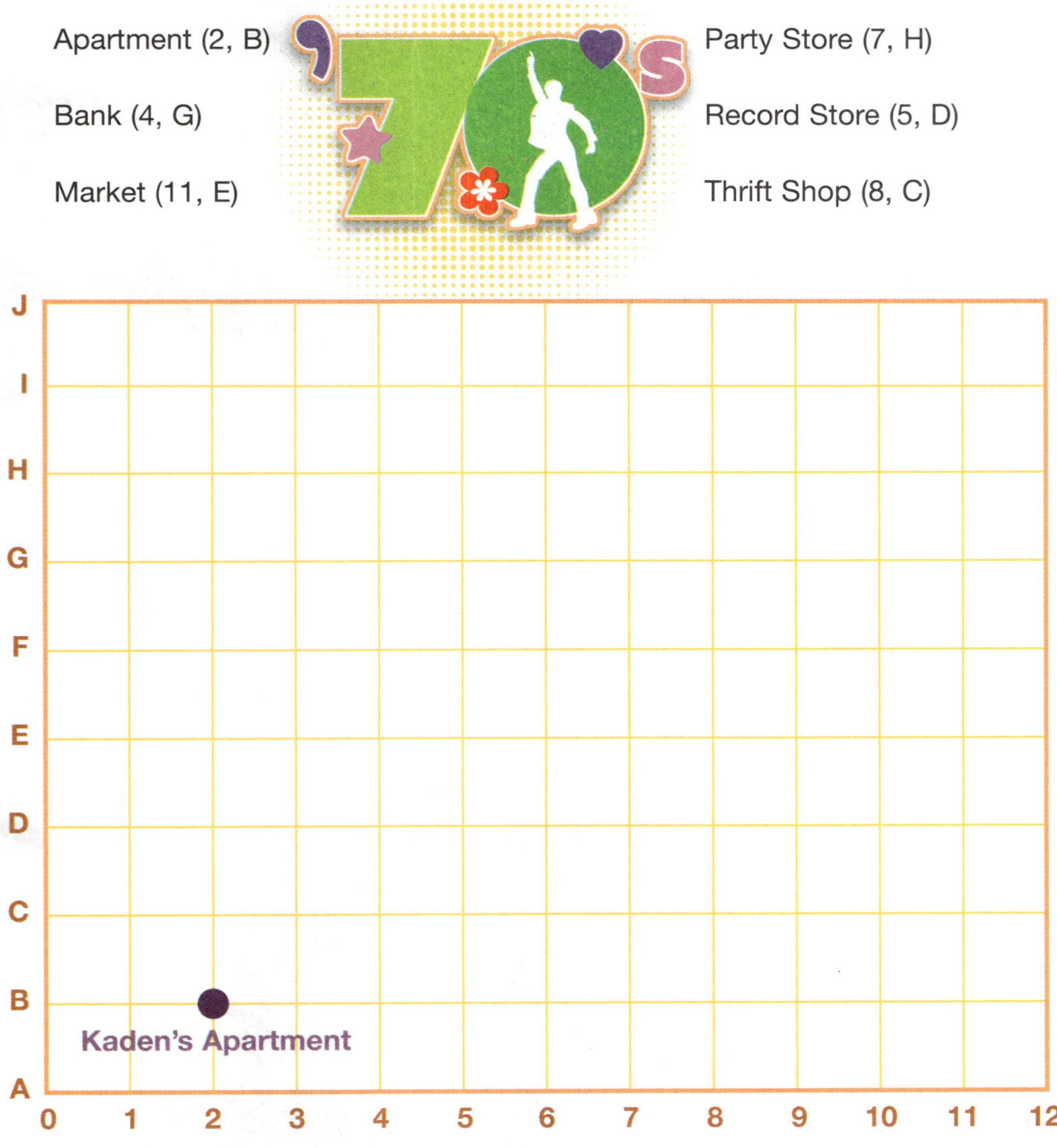

# Follow the directions.

Unscramble and write the letters of each popular food from the 1970s. Then, write the circled letters, in order, to answer the question.

1. **E C S R E P**  __ __ __ (__) __ __  Suzette

2. **Q H U I E C**  __ __ (__) __ __ __  Lorraine

3. **D F O U N E**  Cheese  __ __ (__) __ __ (__)

4. **K C B A L**  __ __ (__) __ __  Forest Gateau

5. **T A P S A**  (__) __ __ __ __  Primavera

6. **E P K O**  (__) __ __ __  cake

7. **L A S D A**  Watergate  __ __ (__) __ __

8. **E H C E S E**  __ __ __ (__) __ __  Ball

**Question**: What pizza topping became popular during the 1970s?

**Answer**: __ __ __ __ __ __ __ __ __

UNUSUALLY FUN READING & MATH GRADE 5    175

# A CLEANER HISTORY

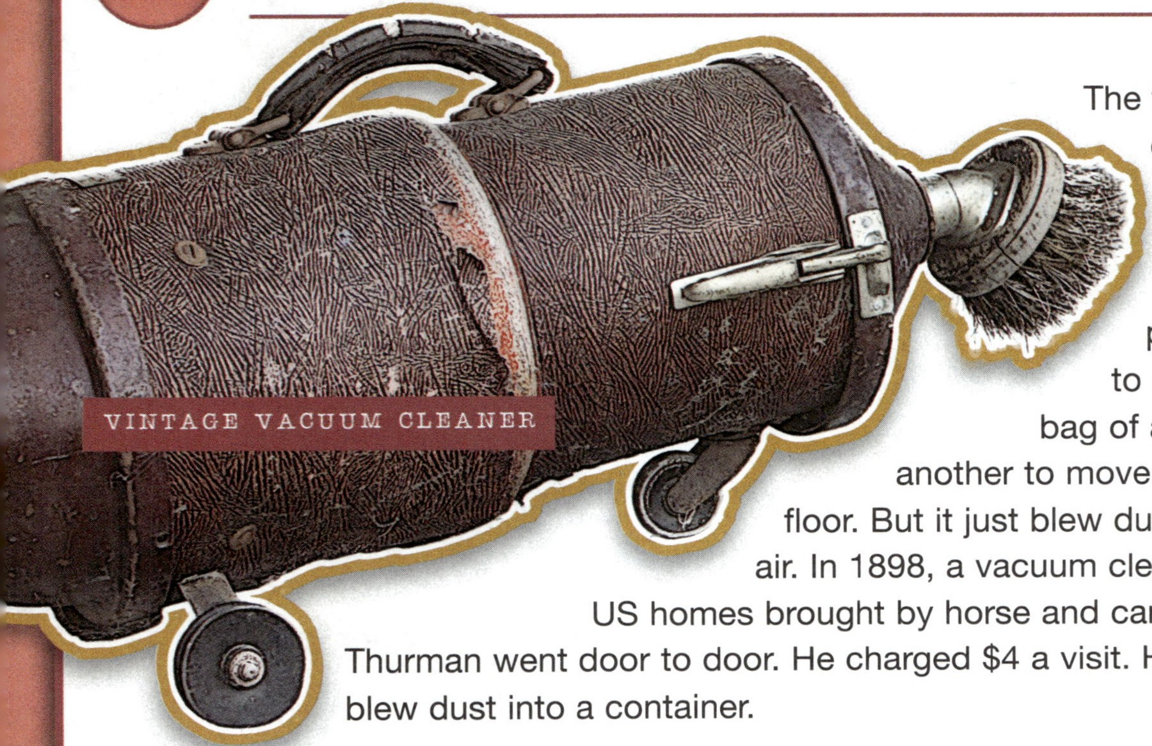

VINTAGE VACUUM CLEANER

The first vacuum cleaner was invented in the 1800s. It needed two people—one to squeeze a bag of air and another to move it across the floor. But it just blew dust into the air. In 1898, a vacuum cleaner came to US homes brought by horse and carriage. John Thurman went door to door. He charged $4 a visit. His system blew dust into a container.

In 1901, a British engineer invented one with a gas engine that sucked out dust. *Puffing Billy*, his horse-drawn cart, was parked outside. Long hoses snaked into the house. In 1906, the *Domestic Cyclone* used water to collect dirt. The first portable vacuum cleaner, more like ours today, was invented in 1908. It had an engine and cleaned with a fan, a box, and a pillowcase.

Every few years, newer and better vacuum cleaners appeared. Today, vacuum cleaners come in all sizes and styles. Some stand upright. Others look like cans. Stick vacuums are long and skinny. Now, we have robotic vacuum cleaners. They clean floors on their own. No horses needed!

ROBOTIC VACUUM CLEANER

## FUN FACT

The world's first cardboard vacuum cleaner was designed in 2011 by a British university student. The cardboard panels from its box pop into place to form the vacuum cleaner body.

**Follow the directions.**

Number the sentences from 1 to 5 to show the order of events in the passage.

_____ 1. "Puffing Billy" was invented.

_____ 2. A vacuum cleaner came to US homes by horse.

_____ 3. The first cardboard vacuum cleaner was invented.

_____ 4. One vacuum cleaned with a fan, a box, and a pillowcase.

_____ 5. The first vacuum cleaner was invented.

**Write or draw a response to the question.**

6. How do you think vacuum cleaners might look 100 years from now?

**Color the dust clouds that contain incorrectly solved problems.**

(Hint: Answers in division problems can be checked by multiplying.)

1. 30)1,865 = 62 r5

2. 44)55,367 = 1,258 r10

3. 98)25,242 = 257 r56

4. 73)8,792 = 119 r21

5. 52)18,804 = 361 r38

6. 19)18,543 = 975 r18

# Follow the directions.

Can you imagine living in a time before some of these important household inventions? Find some of these inventions in the word search below.

**DISHWASHER**  **MICROWAVE**  **VACUUM CLEANER**

**ELECTRIC MIXER**  **WASHING MACHINE**

**REFRIGERATOR**  **ELECTRIC STOVE**

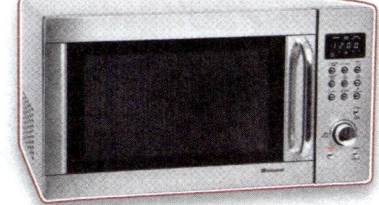

```
W B V Y T K O P L A I U U W I E
V A C U U M C L E A N E R R R D
D K S O K A I L L S O E D E E I
S C D H L S U K G L X Y V F R S
H B F K I D Y J T I D T N R T H
G N F J F N T H M G S R D I Y W
L E I A G F G C M F A V F G U A
O R U S O G I M C B X C G E I S
F Y O D F R R G A C Z M H R O H
B H P M T H E M I C R O W A V E
W G Y C O J W F O X H N Q T Y R
E R E J D K Q D O Z V I W O T K
K L L K D L U S A D B P N R R J
E E L E C T R I C S T O V E E H
```

UNUSUALLY FUN READING & MATH GRADE 5        179

# SQUIRREL CROSSING

WHAT A LIFESAVER!

From his window in Longview, Washington, Amos Peters saw squirrel after squirrel try to cross the street. His office was across from a busy library and overlooked Olympic Way. This busy street ran between large trees and was home to many squirrels. Peters nervously watched as squirrels ran into the road trying to cross, many getting run over.

He asked a pair of architects to work on the problem with him. In 1963, a squirrel-sized bridge was built between two large trees. It crossed Olympic Way. The *Nutty Narrows Bridge* stretched 60 feet (18 m) across. The squirrel bridge was made with aluminum and an old fire hose. It cost $1,000. It was so successful that four additional squirrel bridges have been built in the area over the years.

The Nutty Narrows Bridge is the narrowest bridge in the world and the first one built completely for furry, little acorn lovers. Some visitors have reported seeing squirrel parents teach their babies to cross there. This bridge is family-friendly!

During the holidays, the town adds a small Christmas tree and holiday lights to the Nutty Narrows Bridge.

**Answer each question.**

1. Where is the Nutty Narrows Bridge?

    A. in a park in Washington, DC

    B. above a street in Longview, Washington

    C. in Sydney Olympic Park

2. What was Amos Peters's problem?

    A. His office was too close to the library.

    B. There was too much traffic on his street.

    C. Too many squirrels were run over crossing his street.

3. What was the Nutty Narrows Bridge made from?

    A. steel pipes and rubber tires

    B. aluminum and an old fire hose

    C. steel and concrete

**Write an antonym for each word.**

4. busy _____

5. problem _____

6. narrow _____

Solve each problem.

1. A group of squirrels were collecting acorns. The first squirrel got 2 acorns. The second squirrel got 4 acorns. Each new squirrel always got 2 more acorns than the previous squirrel. The last squirrel got 20 acorns. How many squirrels were collecting acorns?

_____ squirrels

2. Sage the squirrel is storing nuts for the winter. She doubles the number of nuts she has every day for 4 days. On the 4th day, Sage has 72 nuts. How many nuts did the squirrel start with?

_____ nuts

3. Simon the squirrel is also storing nuts for the winter. On the first day he stored 4 nuts. Every day after that he found 1 more nut than the day before. How many nuts will he have stored by the end of the fifth day?

_____ nuts

# Follow the directions.

Help the squirrel make it to the trees safely! Follow the path of prime numbers. (Hint: A prime number is any number greater than 1 that can only be divided by itself and the number 1.)

**START**

| 23 | 3 | 13 | 12 | 121 | 50 |
|---|---|---|---|---|---|
| 24 | 39 | 61 | 27 | 99 | 25 |

| 72 | 91 | 182 | 95 | 139 | 55 | 16 | 8 |
|---|---|---|---|---|---|---|---|
| 4 | 16 | 71 | 11 | 5 | 36 | 42 | 14 |
| 28 | 110 | 19 | 28 | 32 | 6 | 4 | 18 |
| 10 | 81 | 83 | 29 | 37 | 2 | 17 | 90 |
| 40 | 184 | 96 | 12 | 14 | 22 | 43 | 36 |
| 12 | 50 | 39 | 95 | | | | |

**FINISH**

# UNDERWATER HOTEL

If you're adventurous and know how to swim, it may be time to book a room in an underwater hotel. You can find them in China, Sweden, Australia, and the United States, to name a few.

First stop is the Jules' Undersea Lodge just off the Florida coast. It's lovely, but you do have to scuba dive 21 feet (6.5 m) to get to the lobby. It's easier to get to others by boat. Most underwater hotels have above-ground entrances and offer some rooms below sea level. Many have floor-to-ceiling windows that look out into the water. In Tanzania, you will see reef fish and octopi. In China, you may notice black-tipped reef sharks and sting rays glide by. Watch for turtles, sharks, and barracuda in Australia.

WE HOPE YOUR STAY IS "TURTLEY" AWESOME!

These hotel rooms are expensive. One suite in the Indian Ocean costs $50,000 a night! But an underground hotel room in Sweden, 10 feet (3 m) below the surface, only costs $250. Forget the money. Waking up to see a school of angelfish swim past your bed is priceless.

**FUN FACT**

Anyone over the age of 10 can enjoy a sleepover at Jules' Undersea Lodge. The catch is that you must take their Discover Scuba course to get to your room. Room service is then available!

**Complete each sentence with a word from the word bank.**

| entrances | priceless | scuba | underwater |

1. One _____ hotel is off the Florida coast.

2. You have to _____ dive to enter Jules' Undersea Lodge.

3. Most hotel _____ are above water.

4. Waking up to sea creatures by your bedside is _____.

**Write a response to each question.**

5. What might stop someone from staying at an underwater hotel?

   _____
   _____
   _____

6. Where would you build an underwater hotel? Explain.

   _____
   _____
   _____

Solve each problem.

(Hint: To find volume, use the formula V = l × w × h.)

1. Finn is staying in an underwater hotel room. His room is 14 feet long, 16 feet wide, and 9 feet tall. What is the volume of Finn's room?

   _____ cubic feet

2. Isla is also staying in an underwater hotel room. Her room is 6 yards long, 5 yards wide, and 4 yards high. What is the volume of Isla's room?

   _____ cubic yards

3. The underwater hotel has a restaurant. The restaurant is 15 meters long, 17 meters wide, and 5 meters high. What is the volume of the restaurant?

   _____ cubic meters

**Follow the directions.**

Use the information from the passage and the clues below to figure out in which hotel each guest stayed.

1. Eli relaxes in his underwater hotel room and stares out the floor to ceiling windows. He sees an octopus swim by!

   Where is Eli staying? _____

2. Mila is staying at an underwater lodge. She booked an underwater tour during her stay. She has to scuba dive to get to the lobby!

   Where is Mila staying? _____

3. Wyatt is excited for his underwater hotel visit. He eats at the underwater restaurant and watches the sea creatures swim by. He sees a black-tipped reef shark and a sting ray.

   Where is Wyatt staying? _____

4. River saved up $500 so she could stay in an underwater hotel room. She is planning to stay for two nights.

   Where is River staying? _____

# MONKEY ISLAND

In 1979, 1,400 rhesus monkeys were relocated to Morgan Island, South Carolina. It's now called *Monkey Island*. You've probably seen rhesus monkeys. They have short, sand-colored hair and pink, hairless faces.

The monkeys were used for medical research to help scientists understand and prevent human diseases. Some people object to medical testing on animals, and most of these projects have closed. None are done on the island. The animals are monitored and receive veterinary care.

THIS ISLAND IS BANANAS!

About 750 monkey babies are born there every year. Today, at least 4,000 of these noisy animals run around the small island forest. Three-fourths are female. They love to sunbathe on the beach. They also hang out in the trees. They eat from their habitat—roots, seeds, bark, acorns, insects, and shellfish.

You may wish to visit Monkey Island, but visitors are not allowed. First, the monkeys need their space. Also, humans carry germs and diseases that could harm the animals. Last, monkeys are wild animals, and these monkeys run free and are not contained like in a zoo.

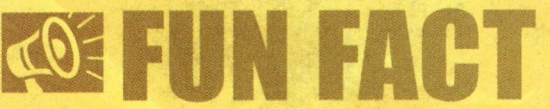

Some exciting video games were created with the island in mind. *The Secret of Monkey Island, Monkey Island 2, The Curse of Monkey Island, Escape from Monkey Island, Tales of Monkey Island,* and *Return to Monkey Island*.

**Complete each sentence with a word from the text.**

1. Monkey Island was first called _____.

2. At least _____ monkeys run around Monkey Island.

3. Scientists have used the monkeys for _____ testing.

**Write the transition words and events from the last paragraph.**

4. _____
   _____

5. _____
   _____

6. _____
   _____

**Solve each problem.**

1. If there are 4,000 monkeys on Monkey Island and $\frac{3}{4}$ are female, how many male monkeys are on the island?

   _____ male monkeys

2. If $\frac{1}{4}$ of the female monkeys have 2 babies each, how many babies would there be?

   _____ babies

3. There are 4,000 monkeys. Of the total number of monkeys, $\frac{3}{8}$ of the monkeys' favorite food is seeds and $\frac{3}{16}$ of the monkeys' favorite food is insects. How many of the monkeys have a favorite food that isn't seeds or insects? Find the answer in number of monkeys and as a fraction.

   _____ monkeys

   _____ monkeys

# Follow the directions.

A veterinarian has come to Monkey Island and needs help figuring out which monkey has a fever. Use the clues to figure out each monkey's temperature.

- Milton's temperature is higher than Maya's.

- Mario's temperature is higher than Millie's but lower than Maya's.

- Millie has the lowest temperature out of all of them.

|        | 98.6° | 99.9° | 100.6° | 101.8° |
|--------|-------|-------|--------|--------|
| MILTON |       |       |        |        |
| MAYA   |       |       |        |        |
| MARIO  |       |       |        |        |
| MILLIE |       |       |        |        |

Which monkey has the highest temperature? _____

# ORIGAMI ON THE MOVE

Do you live in Arizona, Georgia, or Missouri? How about Virginia or Texas? They are just some of the US states that hosted an art show called Origami in the Garden.

This traveling sculpture exhibit is special. You know what origami is—the Japanese art of folding one simple square piece of paper into shapes, such as a crane or fish. In this exhibit the origami sculptures are made of metal. Artists Jennifer and Kevin Box worked with famous origami artists to create the masterpieces. Each design starts out as a single sheet of paper. Thirty-five steps later, it's a beautiful metal sculpture.

The sculptures were designed for botanical gardens. Each outdoor exhibit features as many as 18 large sculptures. They're incredible. Soaring birds and butterflies. Floating boats and soaring airplanes. Galloping horses. Some are as tall as 20 feet (6 m), others as small as a mouse.

The heart-stopper of the show is called "Master Peace." Picture a flock of 1,000 white, stainless steel peace cranes. Five hundred of those cranes are assembled into a 25-foot-tall (7.5-meter-tall) tower. The birds hover in space. The other 500 cranes are scattered one by one in gardens around the world, completing the peaceful scene.

It took three years to produce the Origami in the Garden exhibit and several months building crates for the pieces. The entire exhibit traveled in six tractor trailers, crammed tight from end to end.

**Write a response to each question.**

1. Would you like to visit an Origami in the Garden exhibit? Why or why not?

   _____

   _____

2. The author used words that sound the same—*masterpiece* and *Master Peace*. Explain the play on words.

   _____

   _____

3. Based on what you read, why did the author call the largest sculpture a *heart-stopper*?

   _____

   _____

**Write a synonym for each word from the text.**

4. unique _____

5. flying _____

6. float _____

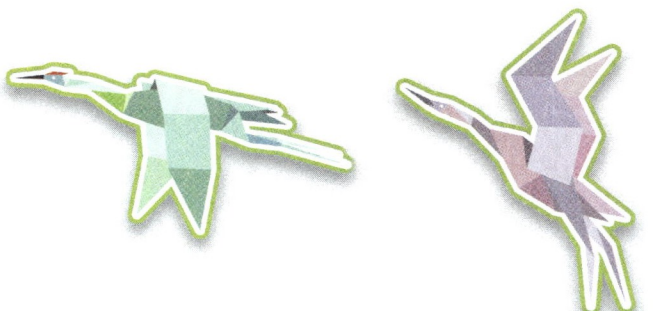

**Solve for the missing angle measure in each triangle.**

(Hint: The sum of the three angles in any triangle is always 180°.)

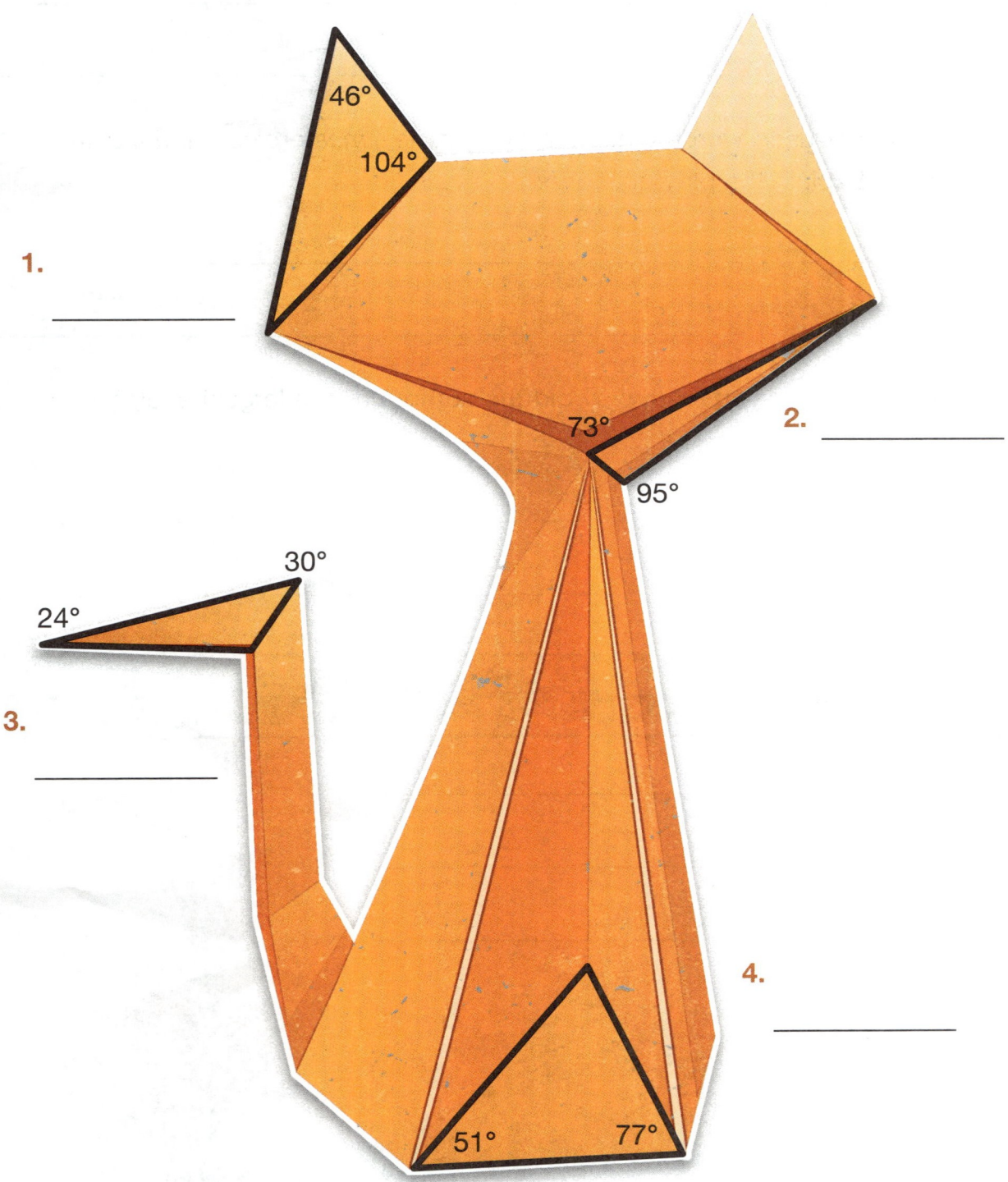

1. _____

2. _____

3. _____

4. _____

# Follow the directions.

Let's create an origami frog! You will need a square piece of paper. Fold along the dotted lines. Fold in the directions the arrows show.

1.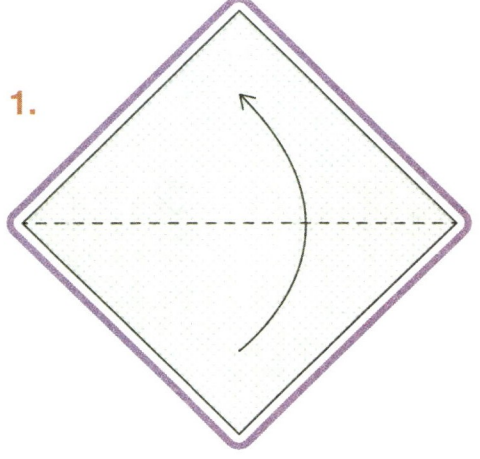

2.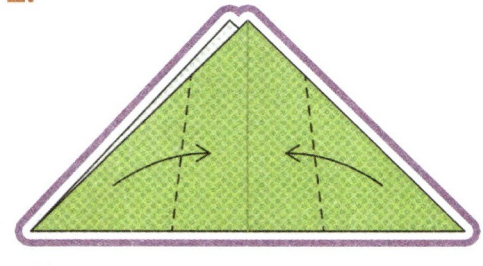

3.

4.

5.

6.

# RAINBOW MOUNTAINS

China's Rainbow Mountains look like a happy artist colored them with all the colors in a crayon box. Tourists flock from around the world to see this sight.

The brilliant reds, yellows, blues, whites, and greens were not painted on the rolling mountains. They were created about 24 million years ago from a mixture of differently colored sandstone and minerals. As Earth buckled over time, the rainbow of layered rock folded and changed.

CHINA'S RAINBOW MOUNTAINS

The site of these mountains is located in Zhangye National Geopark in northern China. Visitors can hike on long boardwalks. The boardwalks are level, making it accessible to people of all abilities. The Rainbow Mountains is listed as one of the most beautiful places in China. Some people call the area "Zhangye's eye candy."

**FUN FACT** — Some think the rainbow colors are not as bright as they look on photos. They think they were touched up to bring visitors. Others think the time of day matters. You'll have to visit to find out!

**Write T for *true* or F for *false*.**

_____ 1. The Rainbow Mountains are in Japan.

_____ 2. The mountains are about 24 million years old.

_____ 3. They were created from a mixture of sandstone and minerals.

_____ 4. Visitors can hike on tree-covered trails.

_____ 5. The park is open to people of all abilities.

**Write one sentence using the pair of homophones from the text.**

6. sight/site _____
_____

**Plot the average yearly temperatures on the graph. Draw the line.**

Jade is planning a visit to China's Rainbow Mountains. She wants to make sure the weather is good when she goes.

| | | |
|---|---|---|
| January 15°F | May 60°F | September 58°F |
| February 23°F | June 67°F | October 44°F |
| March 36°F | July 71°F | November 30°F |
| April 50°F | August 69°F | December 19°F |

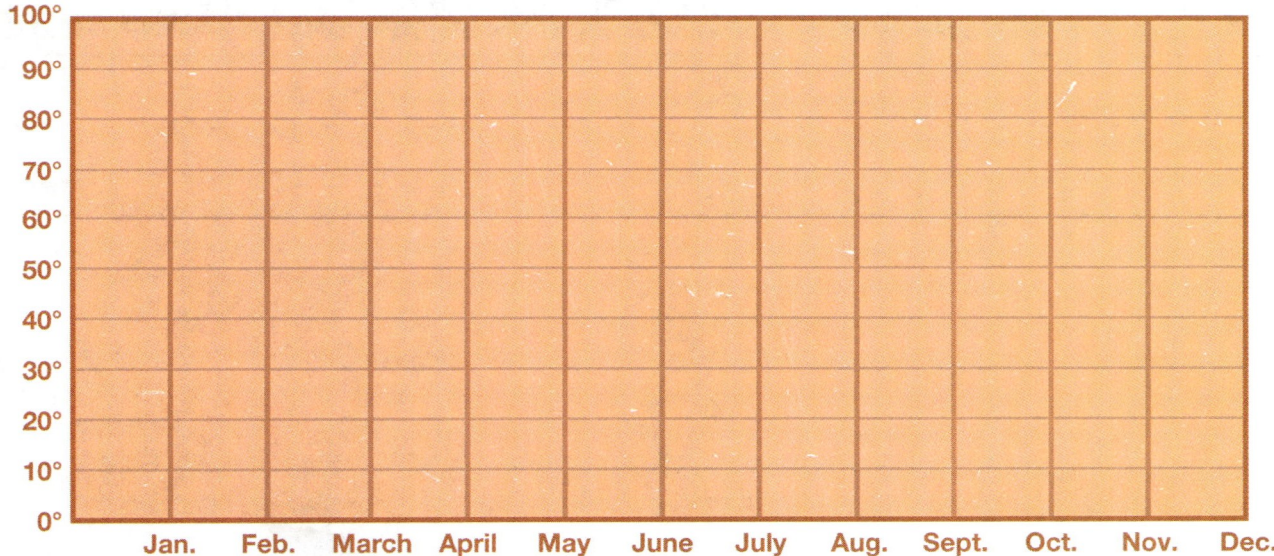

**Use the graph to answer the questions.**

1. If Jade doesn't like the cold, what would be the worst month for her to go?

   _____

2. Jade wants to go in the second warmest month. When should she go?

   _____

3. How much warmer is it in October than November? _____

# Follow the directions.

Determine if each expression is true. Color the boxes that contain true expressions.

| | | | |
|---|---|---|---|
| $0.2 = \dfrac{1}{5}$ | $0.5 = \dfrac{1}{2}$ | $0.25 = \dfrac{6}{25}$ | $0.7 = \dfrac{3}{10}$ |
| $0.75 = \dfrac{2}{5}$ | $0.37 = \dfrac{37}{100}$ | $0.8 = \dfrac{4}{5}$ | $0.65 = \dfrac{13}{20}$ |
| $0.95 = \dfrac{15}{20}$ | $0.12 = \dfrac{6}{25}$ | $0.8 = \dfrac{1}{8}$ | $0.6 = \dfrac{3}{5}$ |

# IT'S RAINING WHAT!?

How many times have you heard someone say, "It's raining cats and dogs!" Is it? Of course not. That's just a saying.

But you might say, "It's raining frogs and toads!" Frog and toad rain has been reported since ancient times. A Greek philosopher reported in the second century that so many frogs rained down, houses and streets were full of them. As recently as 2005, thousands of teensy-tiny frogs came down in a town in southeast Europe. And at least once a year, little silver fishes shower a small village in Honduras. Other weird downpours include maggots, snakes, seeds, nuts, hay, stones, or shredded meat. Even golf balls rained down in Florida.

WHAT HAPPENS BEFORE IT RAINS CANDY?

There's a good explanation for these unusual weather events. Scientists believe a tornado or waterspout can suck up fish from a lake or golf balls from a golf course. How long before they drop like rain? Better carry an umbrella just in case.

 Colored rain is made from the colored dust a storm picks up. Reports tell of yellow, red, and even black rain and snow. In the 1800s, dirty rain turned a flock of sheep black.

**Answer each question.**

1. Frog and toad rain has been reported since

    A. 2005.

    B. ancient times.

    C. the 19th century.

2. What rains down every year on a small village in Honduras?

    A. little silver fish

    B. frogs and toads

    C. golf balls

3. The unusual weather events listed in the text are caused by

    A. angry gods.

    B. tornados or waterspouts.

    C. high temperatures.

IT SPRINKLES!

**Write the true meaning of each weather-related idiom.**

4. It's raining cats and dogs. _____

_____

5. Don't rain on my parade. _____

_____

6. I'll have to take a raincheck. _____

_____

## Solve each problem.

1. It's raining frogs in Newtown! The north side reports a downpour of 4,581 frogs. The south side reports 3,332 frogs. The east side reports 8,075 frogs. The west side reports 926 frogs. How many frogs rained down in Newtown in all?

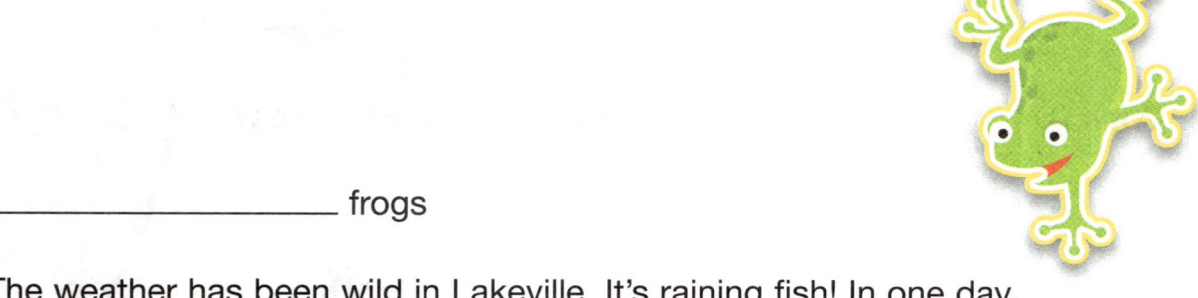

_____ frogs

2. The weather has been wild in Lakeville. It's raining fish! In one day, 12,672 fish rained down. A crew of workers cleaned up 10,697 fish by the end of the day. How many fish are left to clean up?

_____ fish

3. It's raining acorns! The squirrels are happy. In the morning, it rains 7,246 acorns. In the afternoon, it rains 2,585 acorns. By nightfall, the squirrels have eaten 3,112 acorns. How many acorns are there by the end of the night?

_____ nuts

**Follow the directions.**

Frogs, fish, golf balls, oh my! These curious items have all poured out of the sky during strange storms. Imagine you were to witness an unusual rain. What object came down from the sky? Write about the day it happened from your imagined point of view.

_____

_____

_____

_____

_____

_____

_____

_____

_____

_____

_____

_____

_____

_____

# SPACE STINKS!

DO YOU SMELL SOMETHING?

What is enormous, far away, and has a bad odor? Outer space! That's what some astronauts say. Astronauts haven't directly smelled outside their spacecrafts. That would be too dangerous. So, how do they know space stinks?

Space has a lot of weird stuff going on. One explanation for the stench is that when astronauts return from a spacewalk, the part of the spaceship, or the airlock, they enter must repressurize. The chemical reaction that takes place in the air may give off an unpleasant odor.

Another idea is that dying stars, comets, gas planets, and other space materials have their own unique scents. When a star dies it releases a ton of energy. This produces compounds that when combined with air have a certain "tang" to them.

Astronauts compare these scents to many things, including burnt steak, walnuts, brake pads, welding fumes, and burnt almond cookies, just to name a few. Other compounds found in our galaxy can also be found on Earth. Scientists make assumptions about how they smell based on what we know.

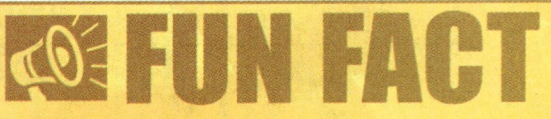 More than 21,000 pieces of space trash larger than a phone are said to be circling Earth right now.

**Write F for *fact* and O for *opinion*.**

_____ 1. Outer space smells like burnt steak.

_____ 2. There is trash in outer space that circles Earth.

_____ 3. Space has a lot of weird stuff going on.

_____ 4. A star releases energy when it dies.

**Write a sentence for each word. Use the part of speech indicated.**

5. produce (v) _____

_____

6. weird (adj) _____

_____

7. assumption (n) _____

_____

**Solve each problem.**

1. Leo found a meteorite on a hike. He is going to sell what he found for $83.75 per gram. His meteorite weighs 2.2 grams. How much money will Leo make?

$ _____

2. Harper sold her collection of meteorites for $5,670. Each gram was worth $450. How many grams did Harper sell?

_____ grams

3. Leilani is buying meteorites for $235.25 per gram. She buys 9.8 grams. How much money does she spend?

$ _____

**Follow the directions.**

Read the clues about planets in our solar system. Write the correct planet name for each clue.

**ACROSS**

3. This familiar planet's gravity isn't the same everywhere. The mountains, oceans, and other aspects of the bumpy surface change the pull of gravity.

4. This is the smallest planet in the solar system.

6. This planet is the hottest planet in the solar system, even though it is the second closest planet to the sun.

7. This planet spins on its side.

**DOWN**

1. This is the biggest planet in the solar system and fifth from the sun.

2. This windy planet is the furthest from the sun.

4. Humans haven't been to this planet, but our spacecraft have!

5. This ringed planet is made of mostly gasses.

# BLUE FIRE

The Kawah Ijen Volcano in Indonesia is also called *Electric Blue Fire*. It is an active volcano and unlike any other in the world. If you look into it during the day, you'll see what looks like a peaceful, blue-green lake. The water is 90°F (32°C). You won't see any wildlife living in or near the water—no fish, no turtles, nothing. It is a living volcano!

KAWAH IJEN VOLCANO AT NIGHT

At night, something mysterious happens. Kawah Ijen looks like it is on fire. Bright blue "flames" shoot into the air. The flames are not lava. The volcano has high amounts of sulfur, a chemical element that is important for all life on Earth. When the volcano's sulfur gases touch the air, they burst into flames. The blue flames can only be seen at night.

Sulfur becomes solid at room temperature. Once the gases cool, bright yellow sulfur rocks remain. Miners break off pieces of the hard sulfur rocks. They carry baskets of up to 200 pounds of sulfur down the volcano where the sulfur is sold. The sulfur is used to make match heads, preserve some foods, and much more. The locals call the sulfur *devil's gold*.

Stay too long at the top of this volcano and the acidic gases and liquids will corrode your items, such as cameras. And, your skin might smell like rotten eggs for awhile.

## Answer each question.

1. What causes the bright blue flames?

    A. burning sulfur gases

    B. the flow of lava

    C. 90-degree Fahrenheit water

2. The word *mysterious* does NOT mean

    A. puzzling.

    B. relating to a mystery.

    C. brightly colored.

3. How have local people made an income from the volcano?

    A. They swim in the lake.

    B. They mine sulfur rocks.

    C. They take photos of the blue flames.

## Write a synonym for each word.

4. remain _____

5. burst _____

6. suffer _____

Write the best unit to measure each object.

> 12 inches = 1 foot    36 inches = 1 yard
>
> 3 feet = 1 yard    5,280 feet = 1 mile

1. The length of a piece of sulfur.

   _____

2. The distance from the bottom of the Kawah Ijen Volcano to the top.

   _____

3. The distance from one side of the crater lake to the other.

   _____

4. The length of the pole between a sulfur miner's baskets.

   _____

# Follow the directions.

The beautiful turquoise crater lake at the Kawah Ijen Volcano looks like the perfect place for a dip. Use the code to reveal why the looks of this lake are deceiving!

| 1 | 2 | 3 | 4 | 5 | 6 | 7 | 8 | 9 | 10 | 11 | 12 | 13 |
|---|---|---|---|---|---|---|---|---|----|----|----|----|
| A | B | C | D | E | F | G | H | I | J  | K  | L  | M  |

| 14 | 15 | 16 | 17 | 18 | 19 | 20 | 21 | 22 | 23 | 24 | 25 | 26 |
|----|----|----|----|----|----|----|----|----|----|----|----|----|
| N  | O  | P  | Q  | R  | S  | T  | U  | V  | W  | X  | Y  | Z  |

__ __   __ __   __ __ __
9 20    9 19    20 8 5

__ __ __ __ __ __ ,
23 15 18 12 4 19

__ __ __ __ __ __ __
2  9  7  7  5 19 20

__ __ __ __ __ __   __ __ __ __.
1  3  9  4  9  3    12 1 11 5

# THE LONELIEST PLACE

Point Nemo has nothing to do with the sweet clownfish who lives in a sea anemone with his father. It's a place. It's the spot in the ocean that is furthest from land than any other. In fact, you are closer to the International Space Station—258 miles (416 km) up—at Point Nemo than dry land.

Point Nemo is 1,670 miles (2,688 km) from the nearest place you could sit down. You can't actually visit. There's nothing there! It's just an invisible spot in the enormous Southern Ocean. It is the place hardest to get to on Earth.

Point Nemo is known as a spacecraft cemetery. It's considered the perfect crash site for satellites and other space vehicles coming in from outer space. About 300 American, European, and Japanese spacecraft have crashed there.

The water there holds next to nothing else. But some years ago, scientists picked up a mysterious sound. Named *the Bloop*, it was louder than a blue whale's voice. Everyone was excited until they learned it was just the sound of a giant iceberg cracking. Nope, there's no one home at Point Nemo.

A GIANT SQUID ATTACKS THE NAUTILUS OF CAPTAIN NEMO, AN ILLUSTRATION FROM JULES VERNE'S NOVEL.

**FUN FACT** Point Nemo was named after Captain Nemo in the book *Twenty Thousand Leagues Under the Seas* by Jules Verne. In Latin, *nemo* means "no one."

**Match each word to its definition.**

1. sea anemone                                    graveyard

2. enormous                                       a spacecraft sent into orbit

3. cemetery                                       marine life that resembles a flower

4. satellite                                      huge

**Write a response to each question.**

5. What is the most surprising thing you learned about Point Nemo?

_____

_____

6. Would you want to visit Point Nemo? Explain.

_____

_____

_____

Write the best unit of measure for each problem.

> 1 meter = 39.37 inches    100 centimeters = 1 meter
>
> 10 millimeters = 1 centimeter    1,000 meters = 1 kilometer

1. The distance from Point Nemo to land

   _____

2. The length of a fishing boat

   _____

3. The length of a blue whale

   _____

4. The length of a clownfish

   _____

**Follow the directions.**

Make your way through the maze from space to Point Nemo. Write the letters you cross in order on the lines below to finish the fun fact.

NASA is retiring the International

___ ___ ___ ___ ___

___ ___ ___ ___ ___ ___ ___

in 2030 and they plan to crash it into Point Nemo.

# Answer Key

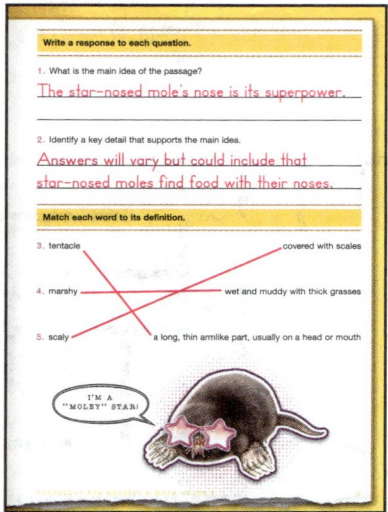

Page 5

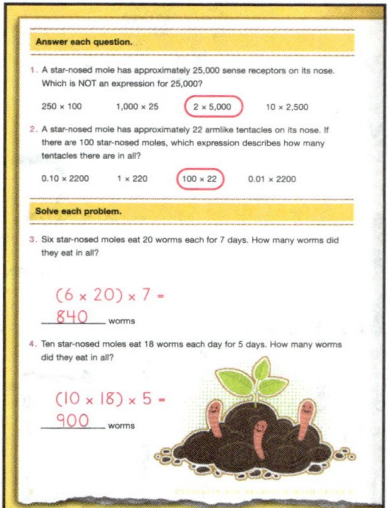

Page 6

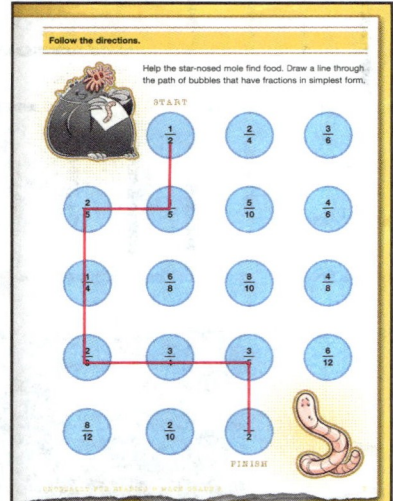

Page 7

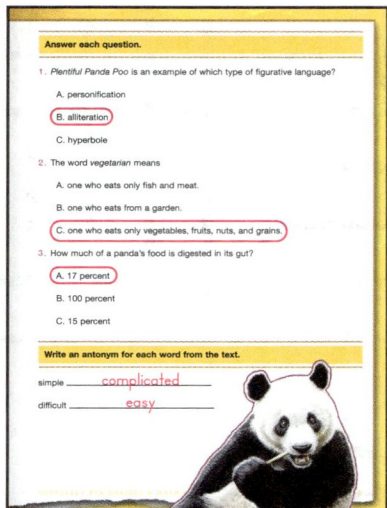

Page 9

# Answer Key

Page 10

Page 11

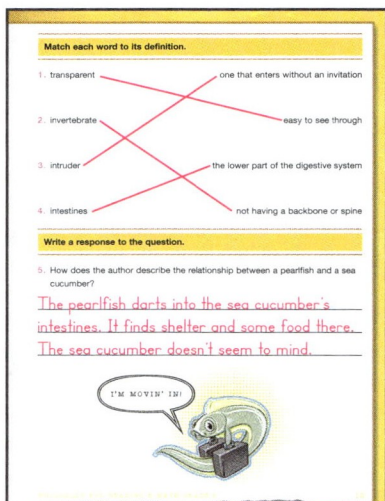
Page 13

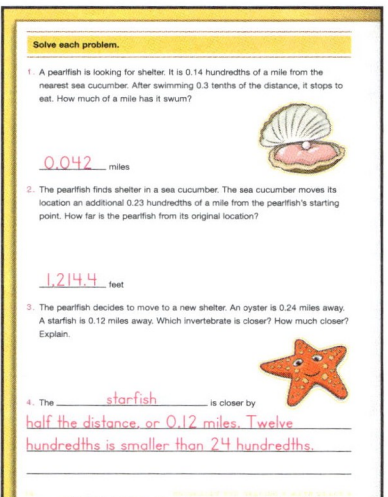
Page 14

# Answer Key

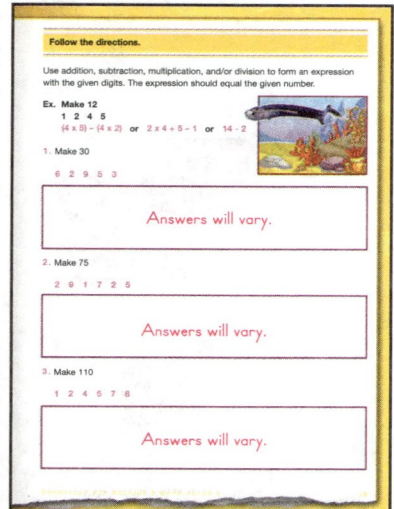

Page 15

Page 17

Page 18

Page 19

# Answer Key

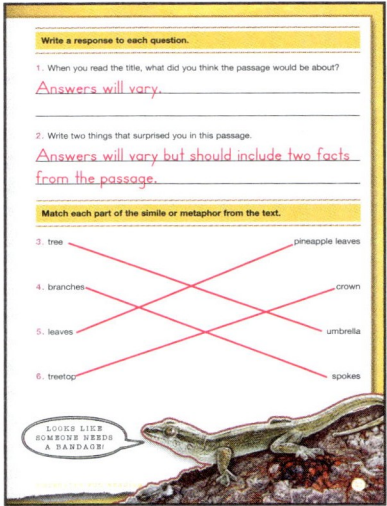

Page 21

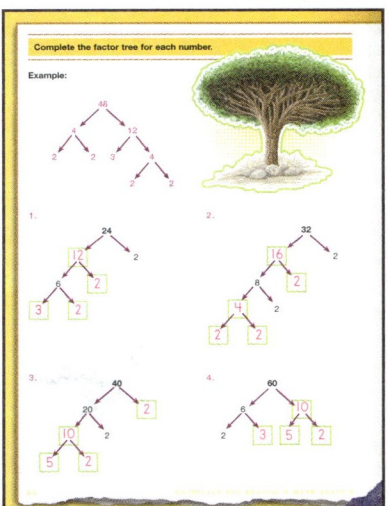

Page 22

Page 23

Page 25

# Answer Key

Page 26

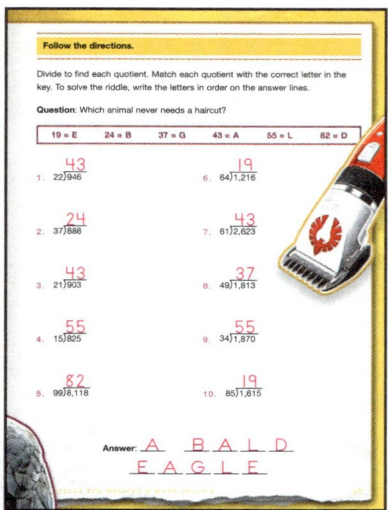

Page 27

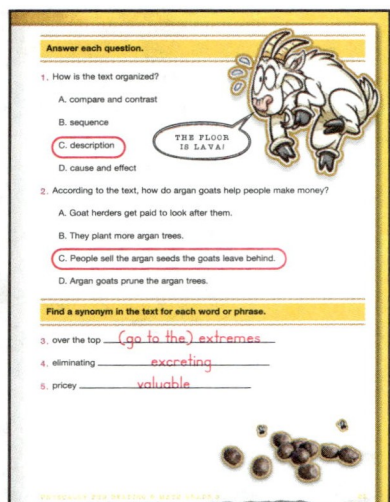

Page 29

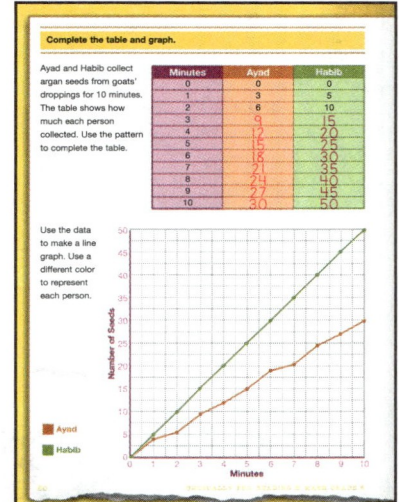

Page 30

# Answer Key

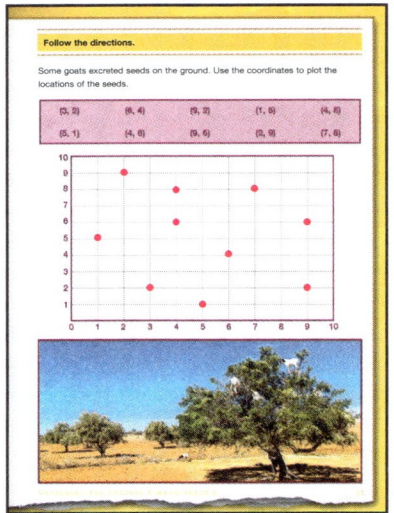
Page 31

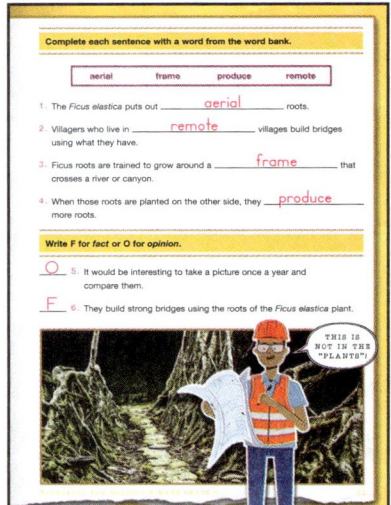
Page 33

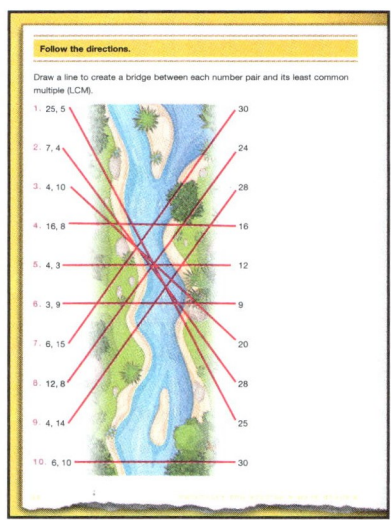
Page 34

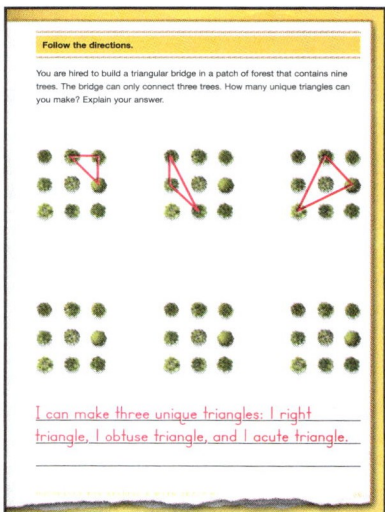
Page 35

# Answer Key

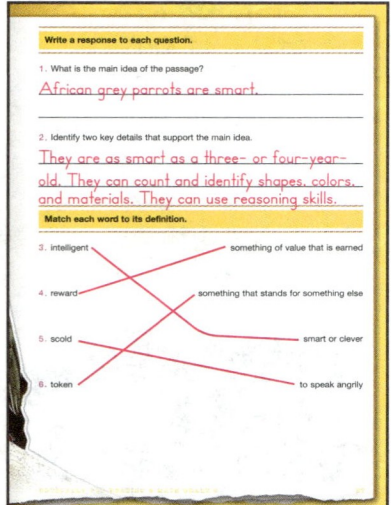

Page 37

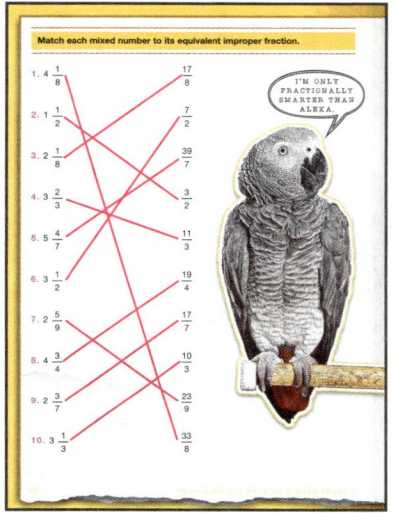

Page 38

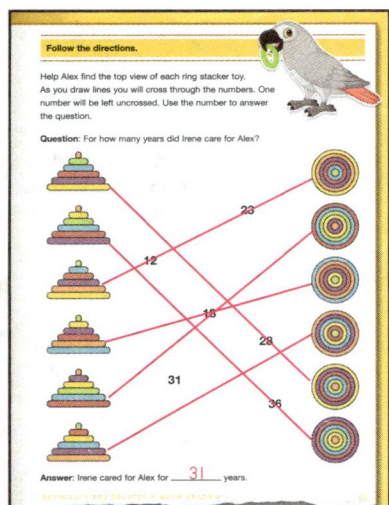

Page 39

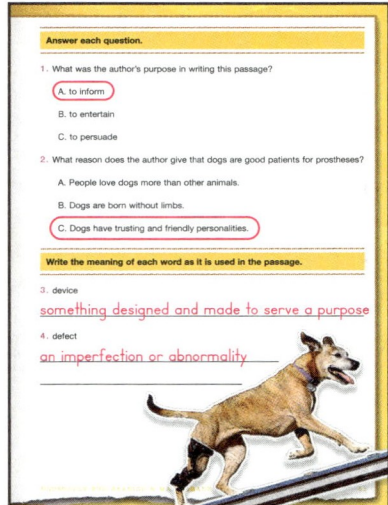

Page 41

# Answer Key

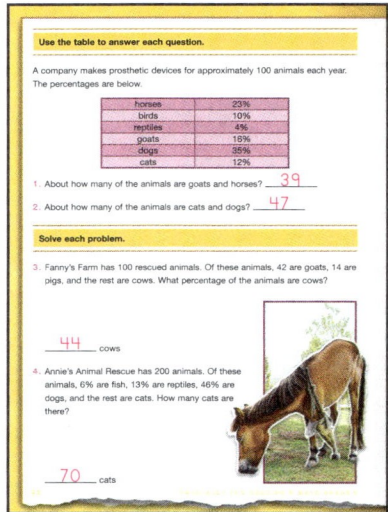

Page 42

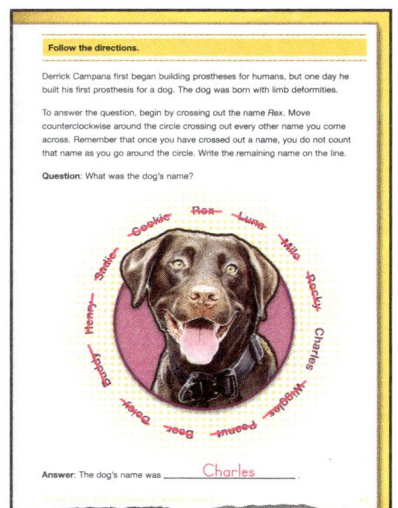

Page 43

Page 45

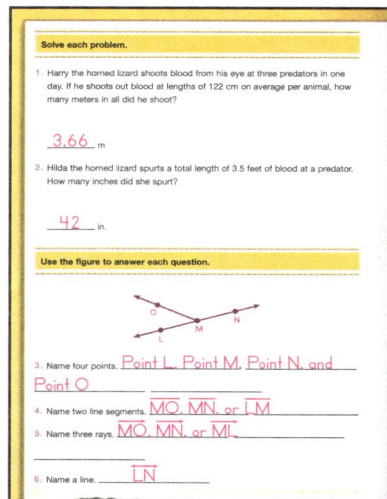

Page 46

# Answer Key

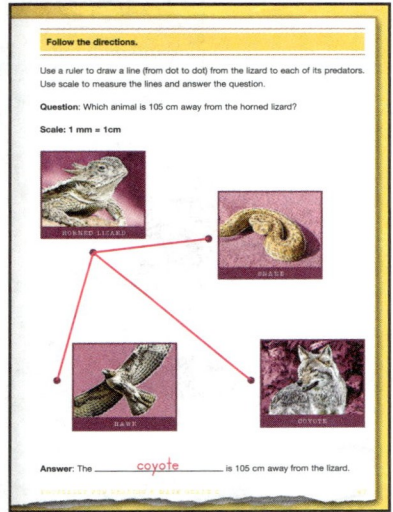

Page 47

Page 49

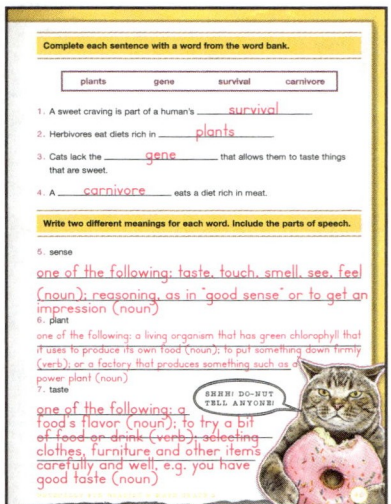

Page 50

Page 51

# Answer Key

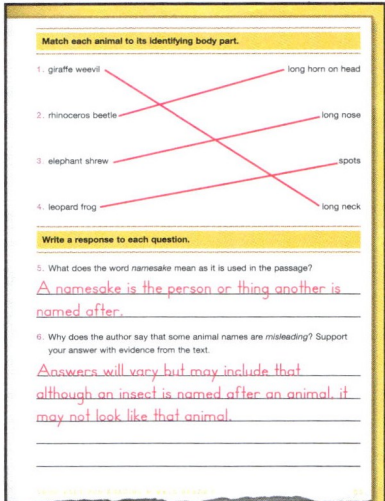

Page 53

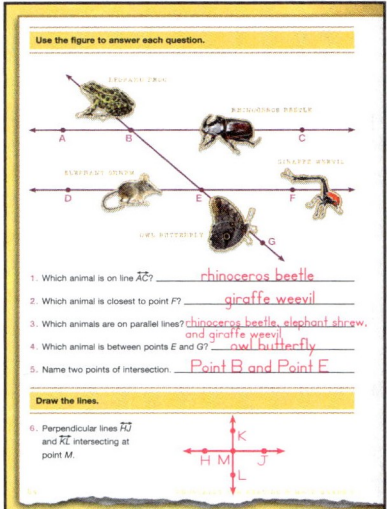

Page 54

Page 55

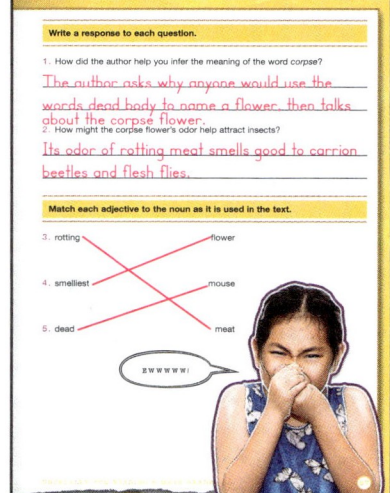

Page 57

# Answer Key

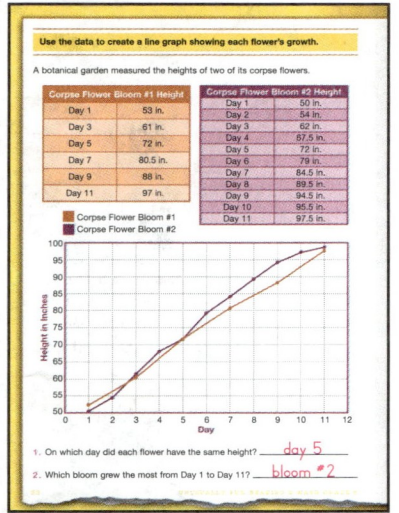
Page 58

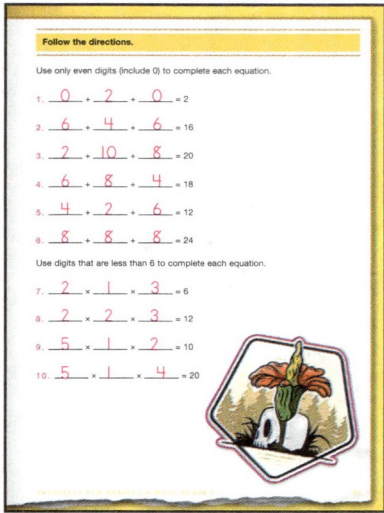
Page 59

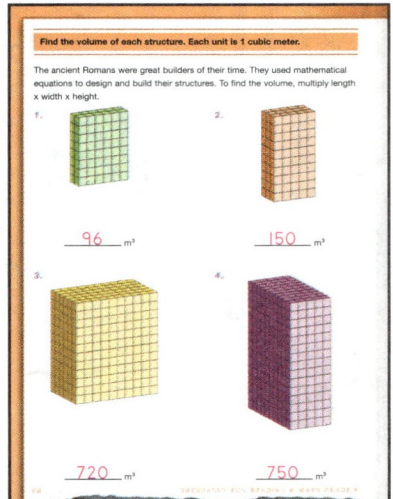
Page 61

Page 62

# Answer Key

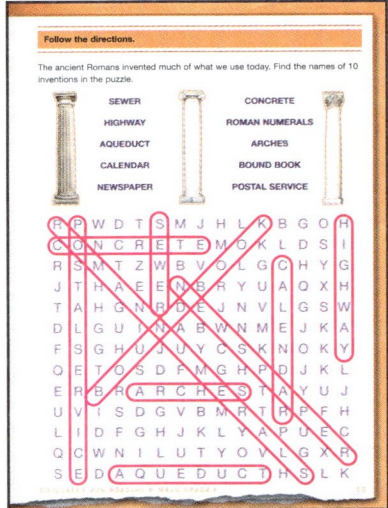
Page 63

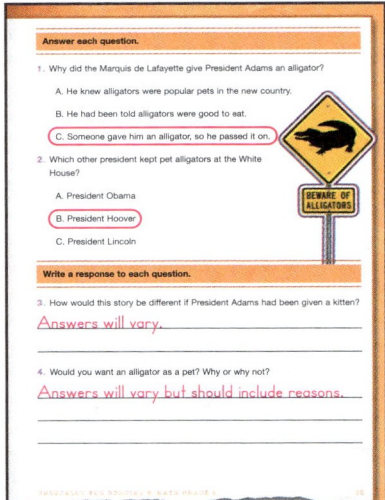
Page 65

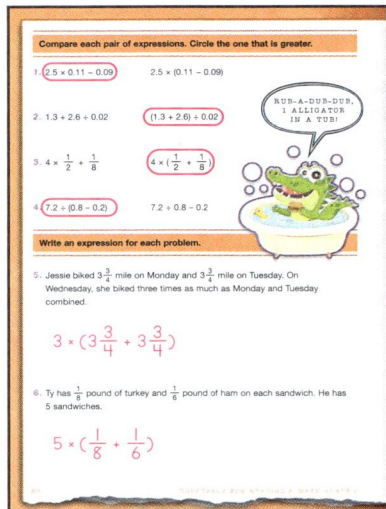
Page 66

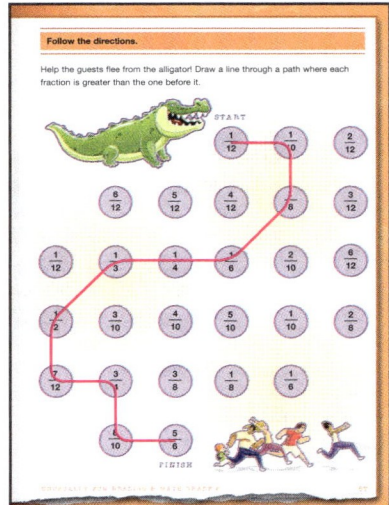
Page 67

# Answer Key

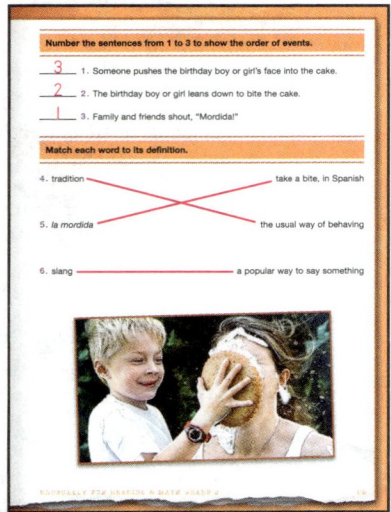

Page 69

Page 70

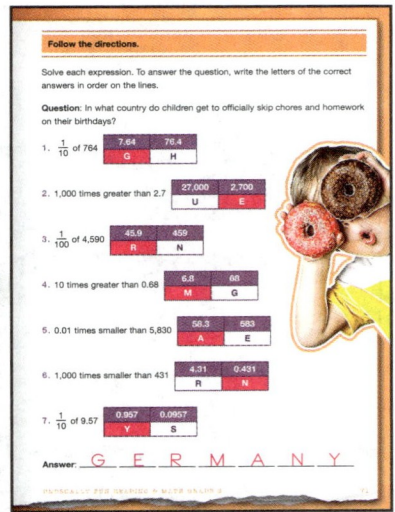

Page 71

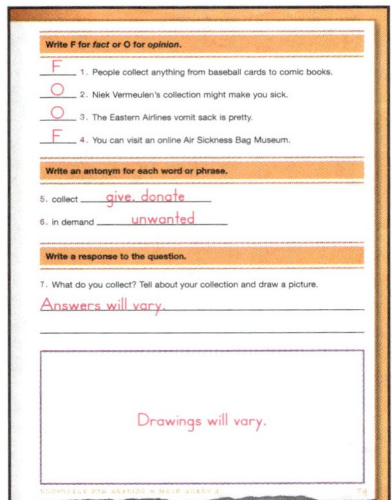

Page 73

# Answer Key

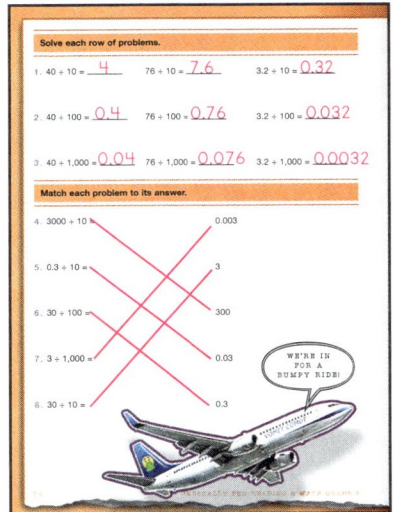

Page 74

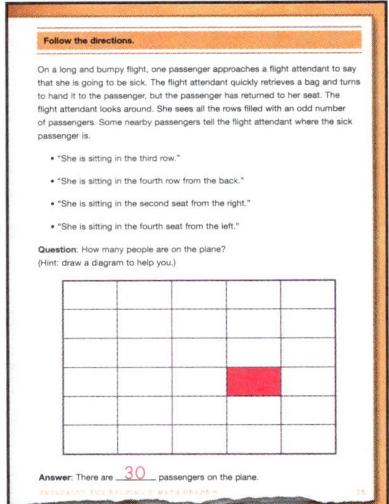

Page 75

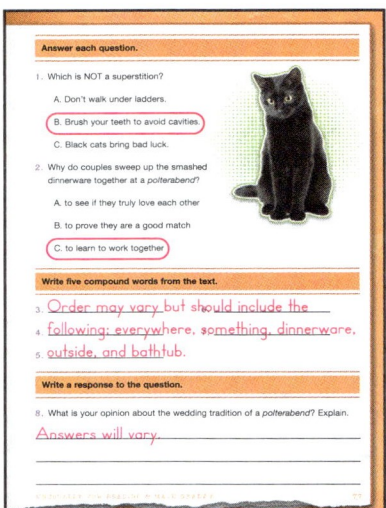

Page 77

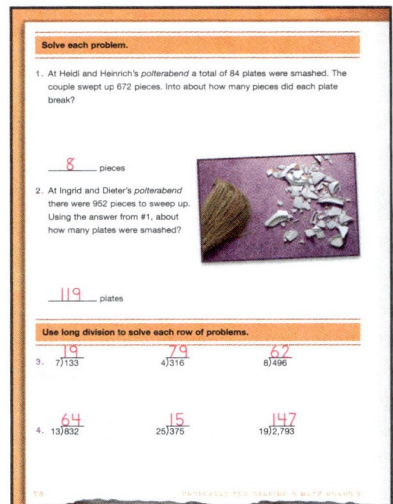

Page 78

# Answer Key

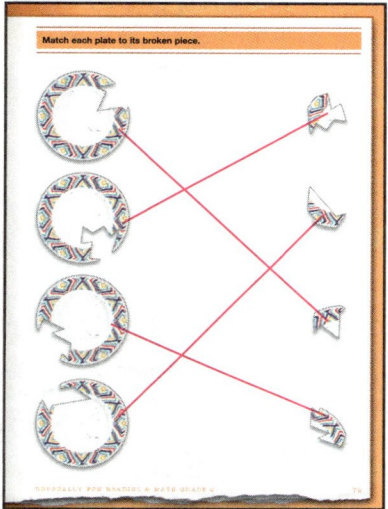

Page 79

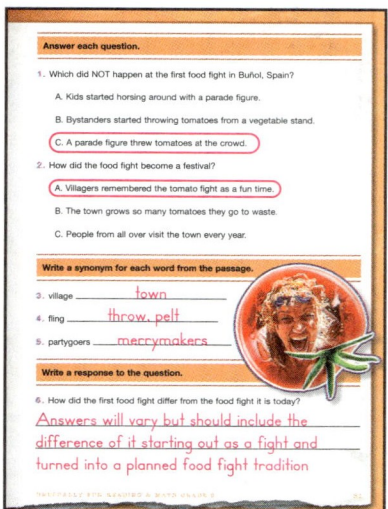

Page 81

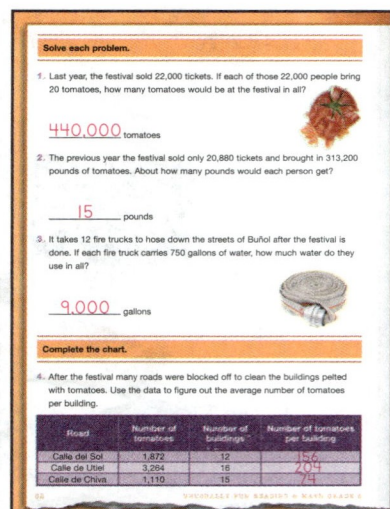

Page 82

Page 83

# Answer Key

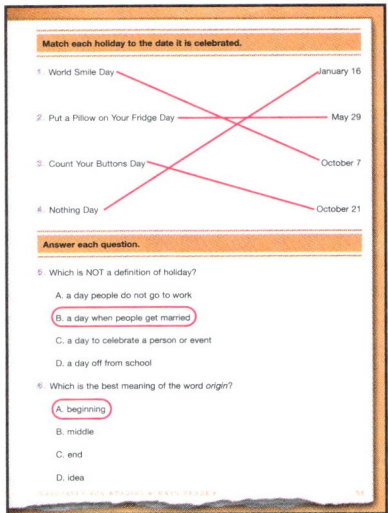

Page 85

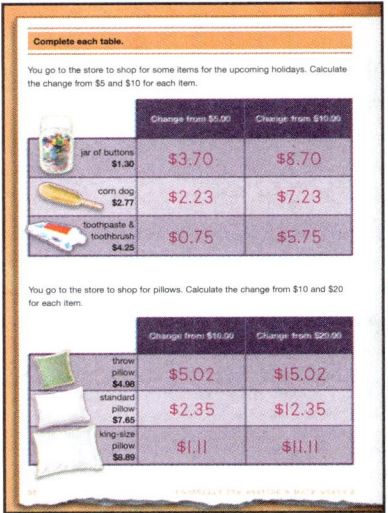

Page 86

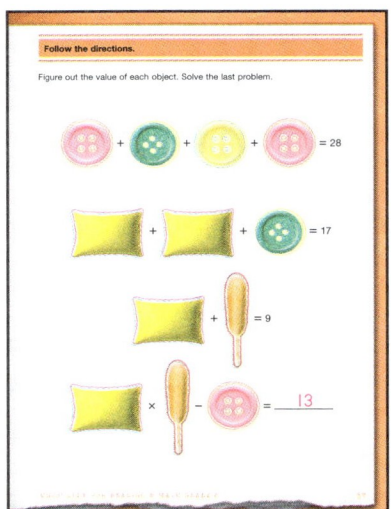

Page 87

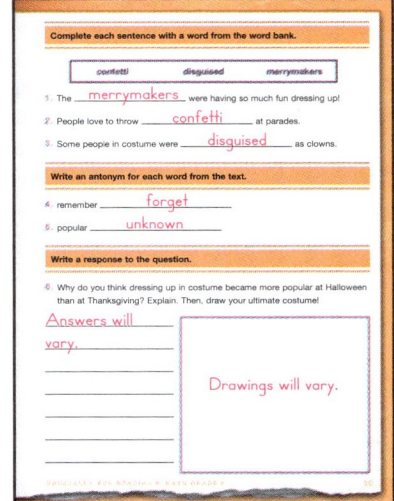

Page 89

# Answer Key

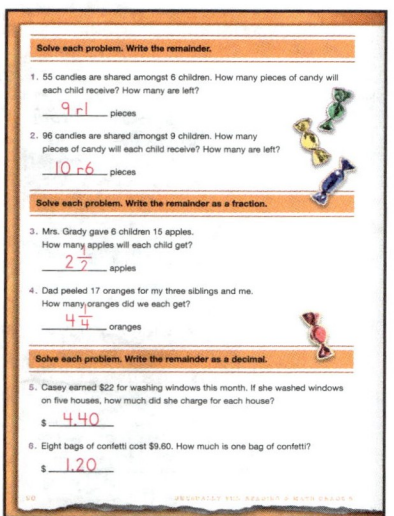

Page 90

Page 91

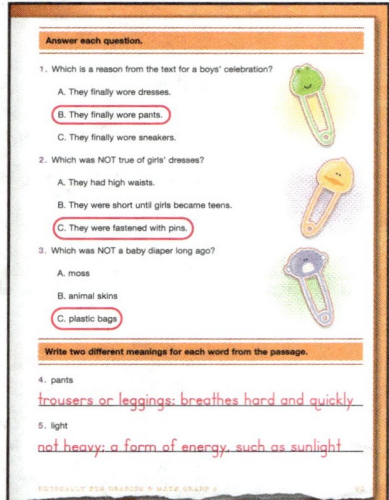

Page 93

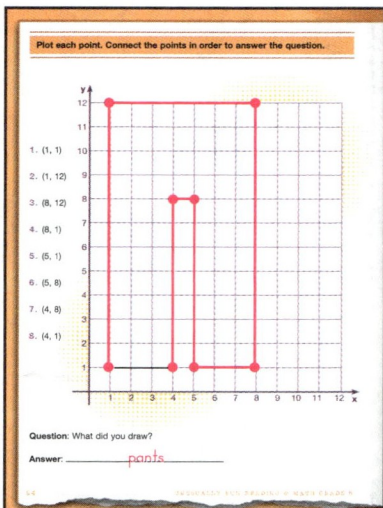

Page 94

# Answer Key

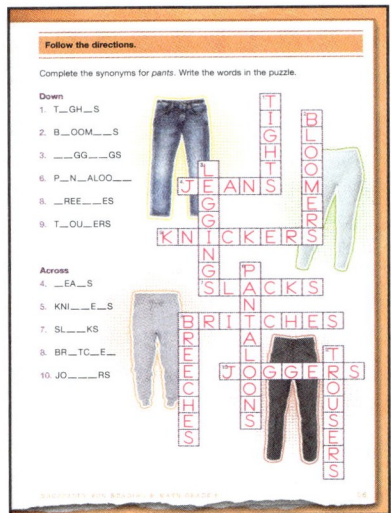

Page 95

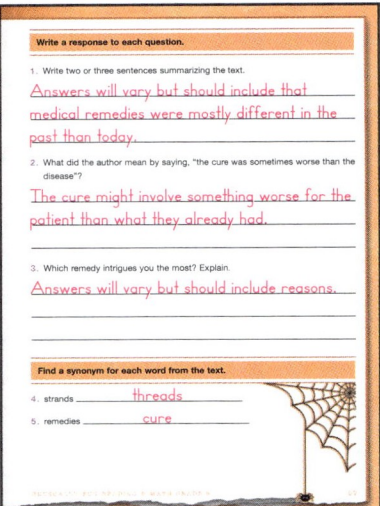

Page 97

Page 98

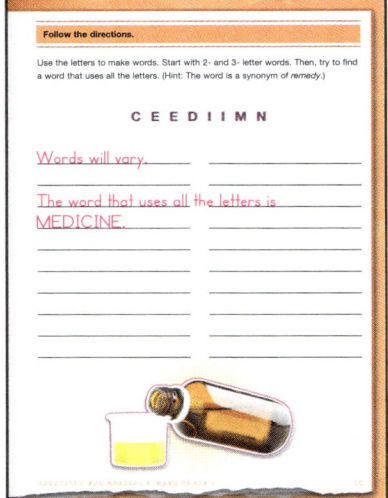

Page 99

# Answer Key

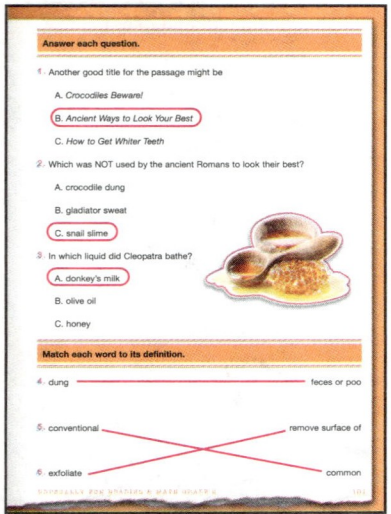

Page 101

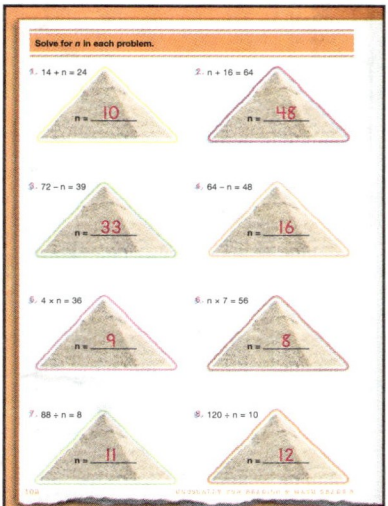

Page 102

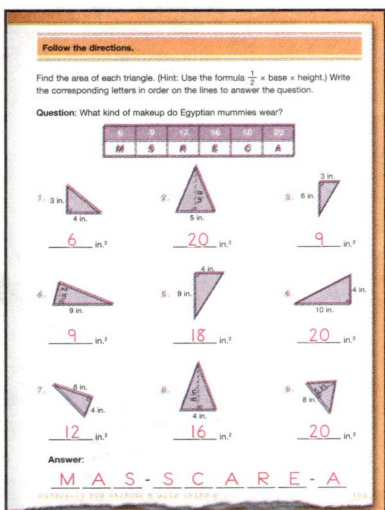

Page 103

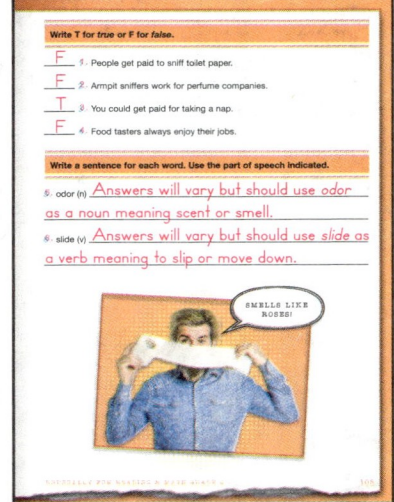

Page 105

# Answer Key

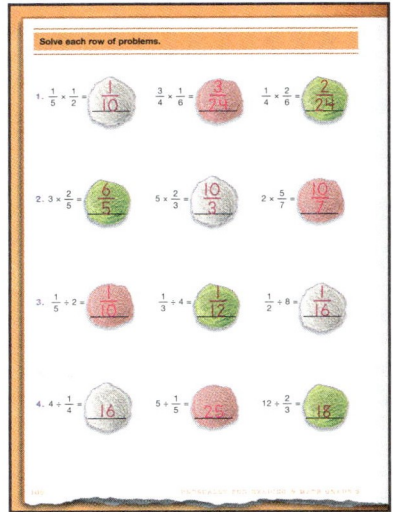

Page 106

Page 107

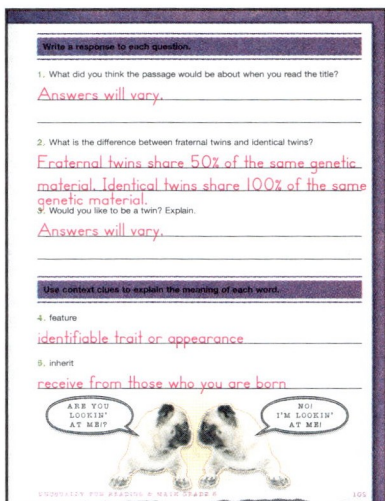

Page 109

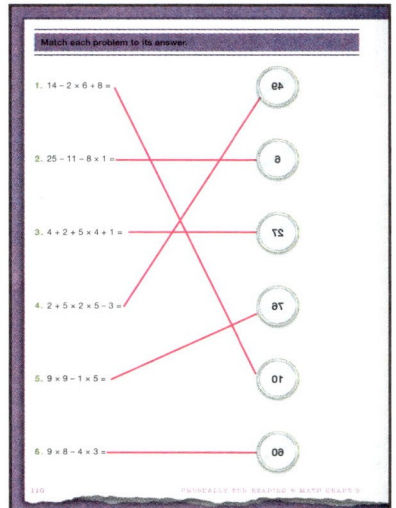

Page 110

# Answer Key

Page 111

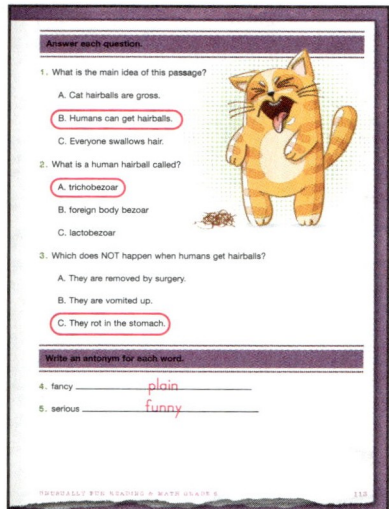

Page 113

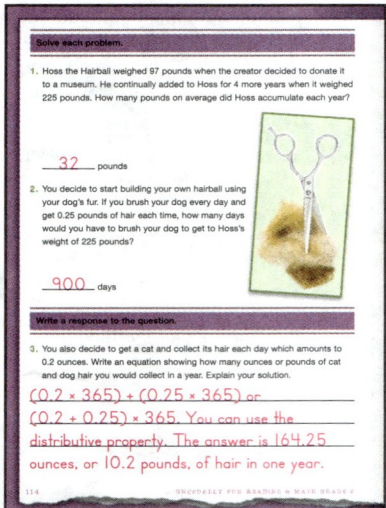

Page 114

Page 115

# Answer Key

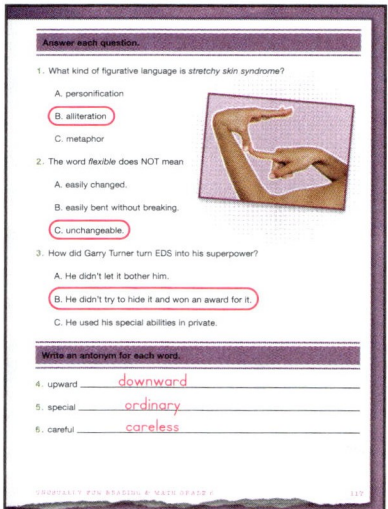
Page 117

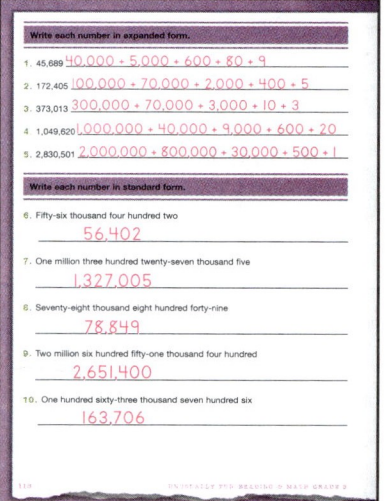
Page 118

Page 119

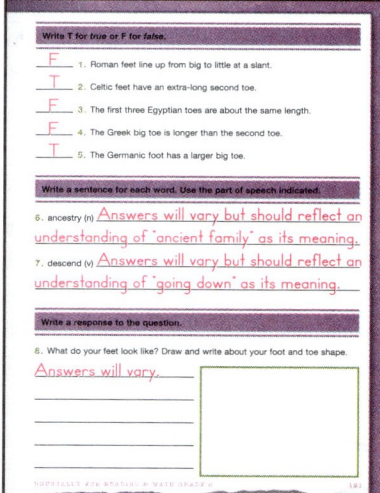
Page 121

# Answer Key

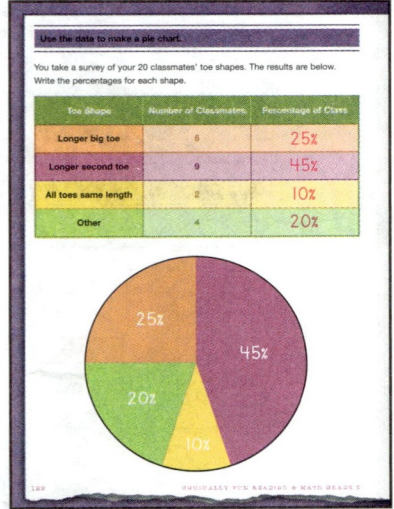
Page 122

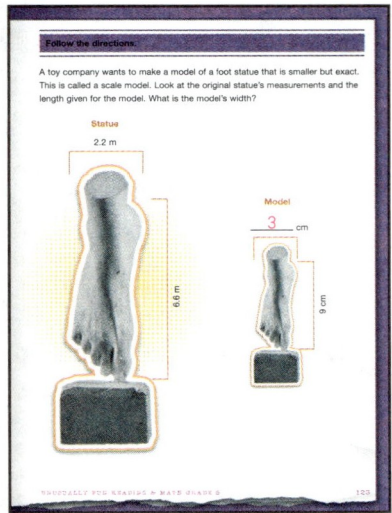
Page 123

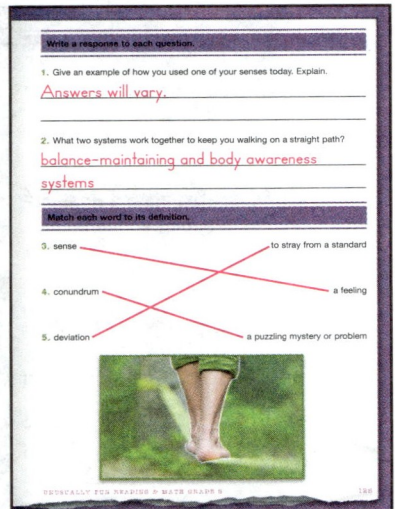
Page 125

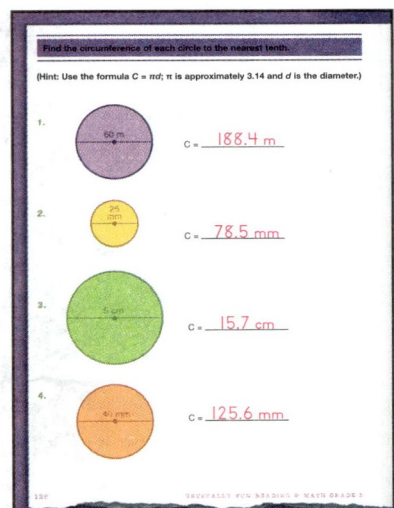
Page 126

# Answer Key

Page 127

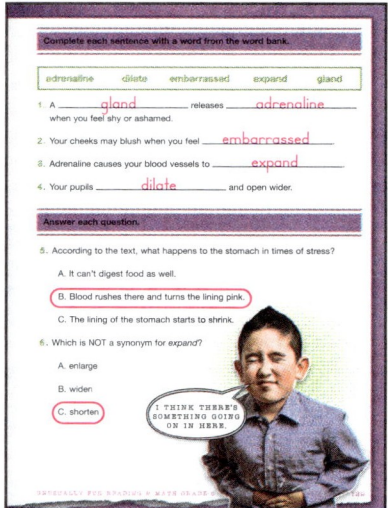

Page 129

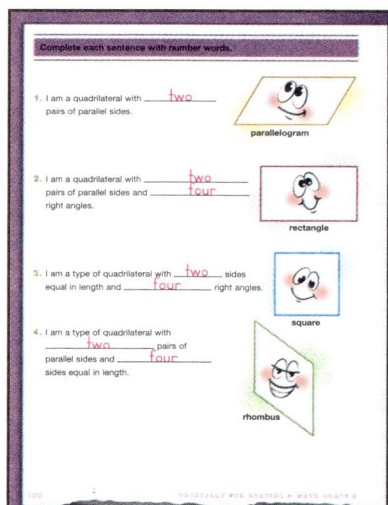

Page 130

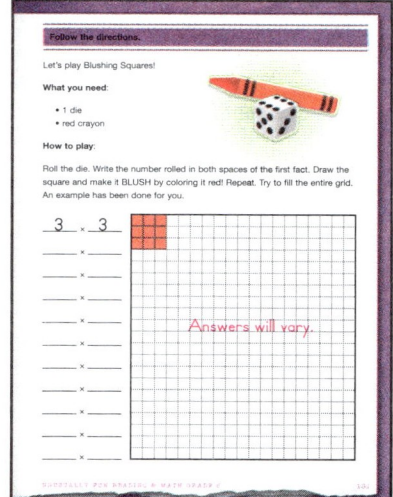

Page 131

# Answer Key

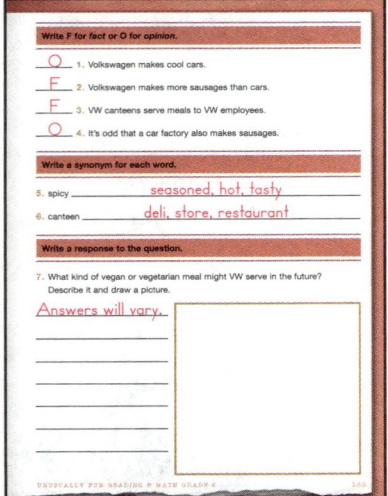

Page 133

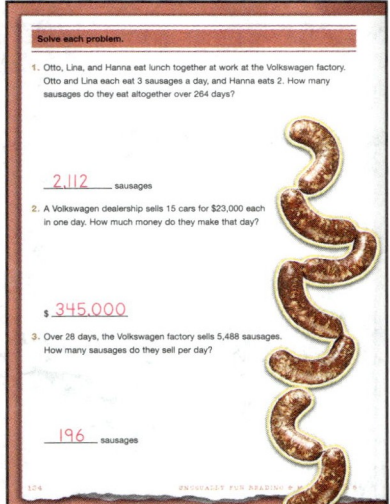

Page 134

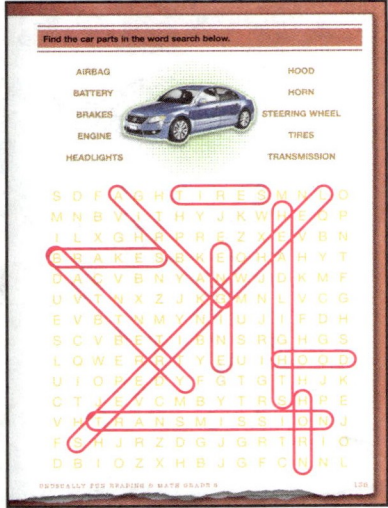

Page 135

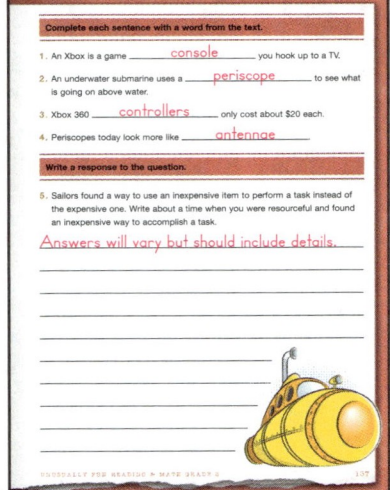

Page 137

# Answer Key

Page 138

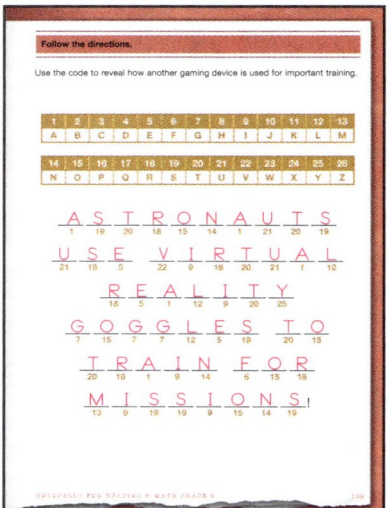

Page 139

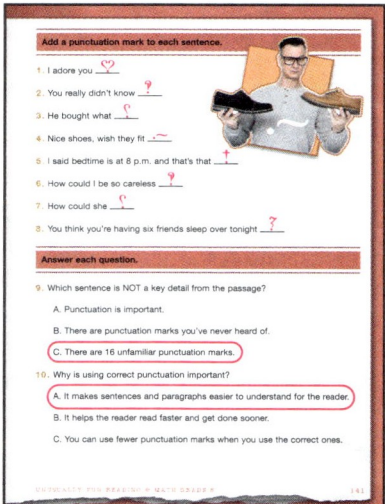

Page 141

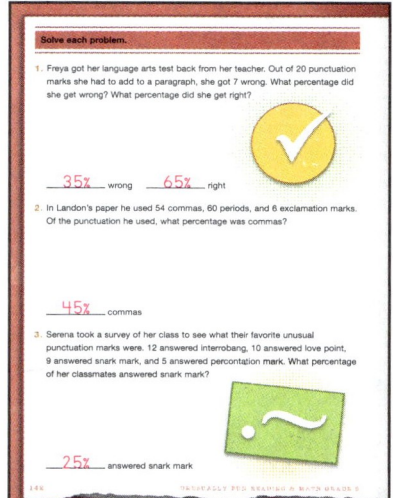

Page 142

# Answer Key

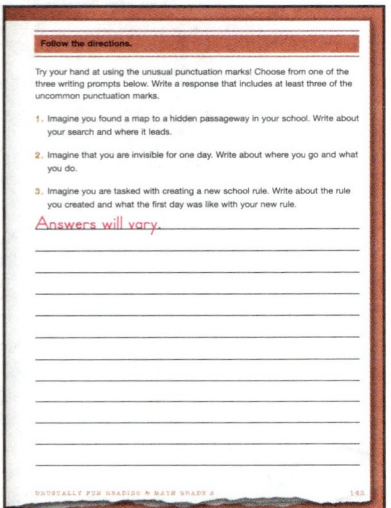

Page 143

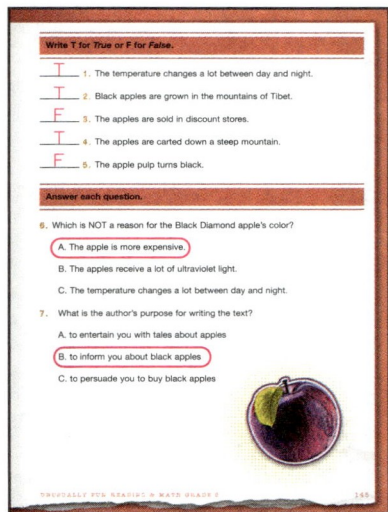

Page 145

Page 146

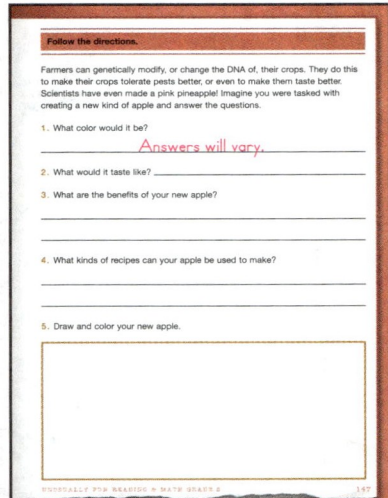

Page 147

# Answer Key

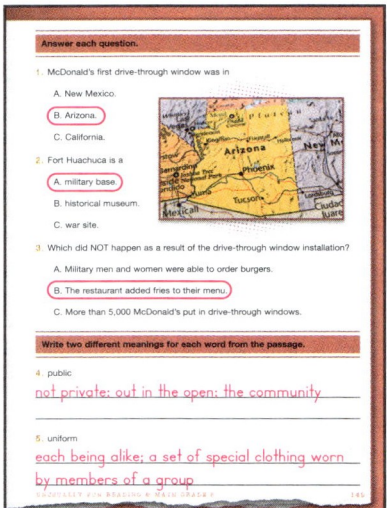
Page 149

Page 150

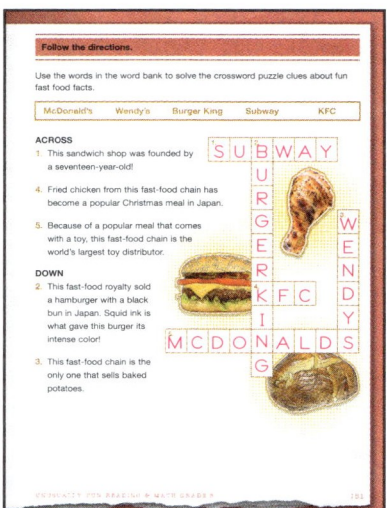
Page 151

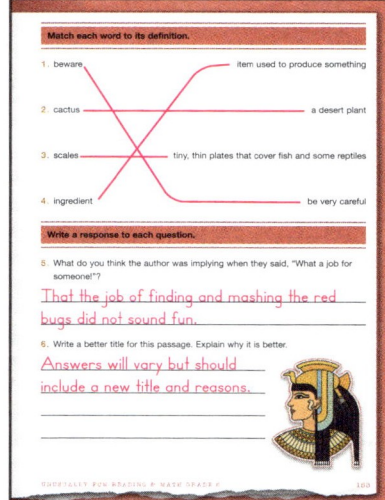
Page 153

# Answer Key

Page 154

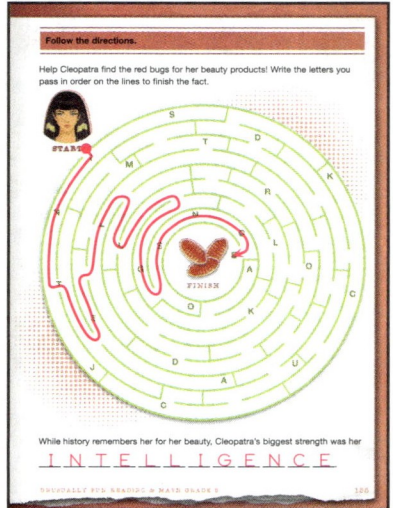

Page 155

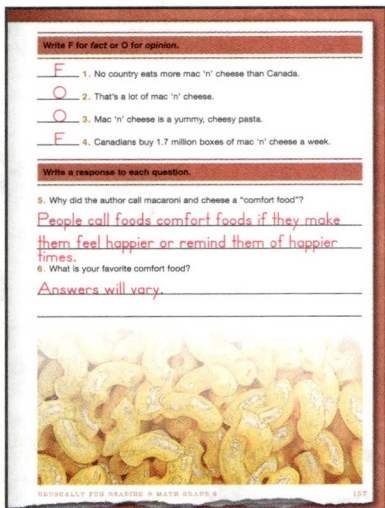

Page 157

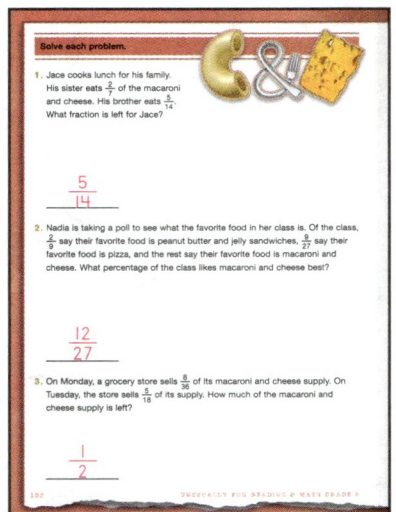

Page 158

# Answer Key

Page 159

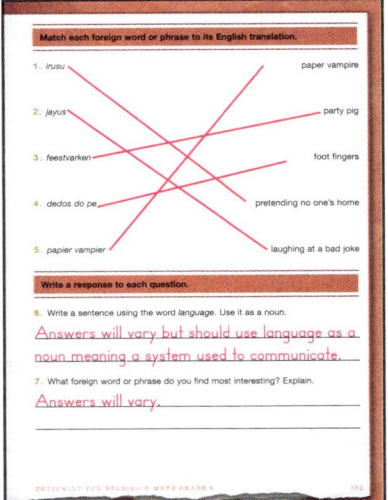

Page 161

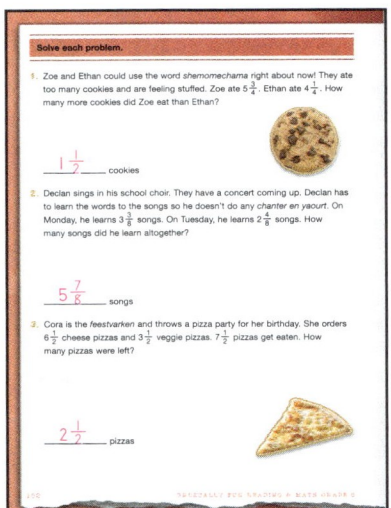

Page 162

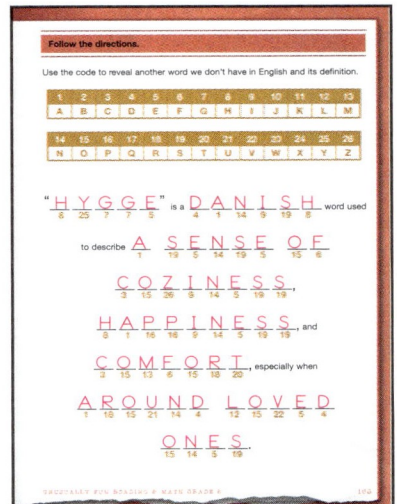

Page 163

# Answer Key

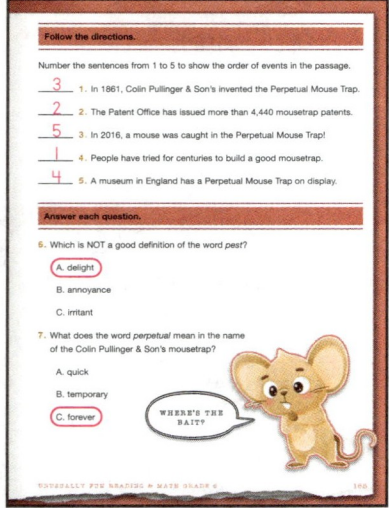
Page 165

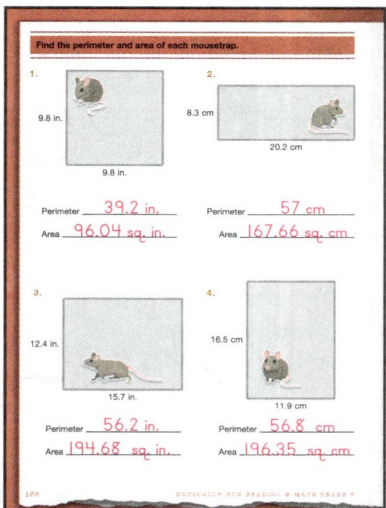
Page 166

Page 167

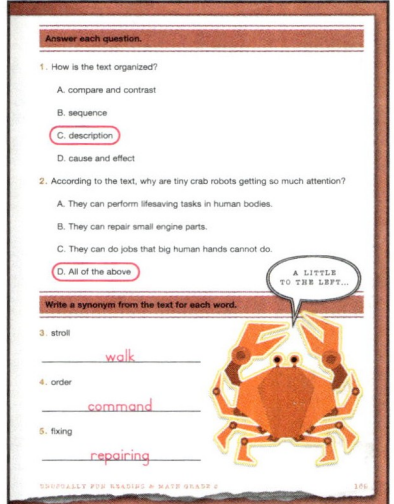
Page 169

# Answer Key

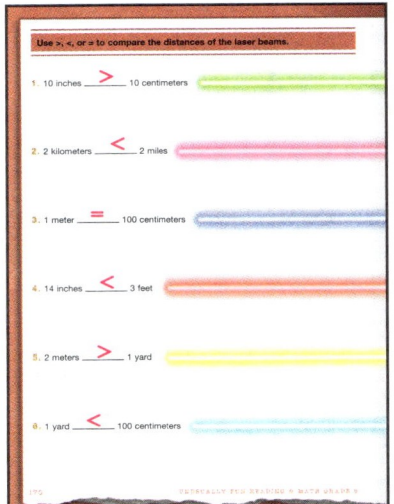

Page 170

Page 171

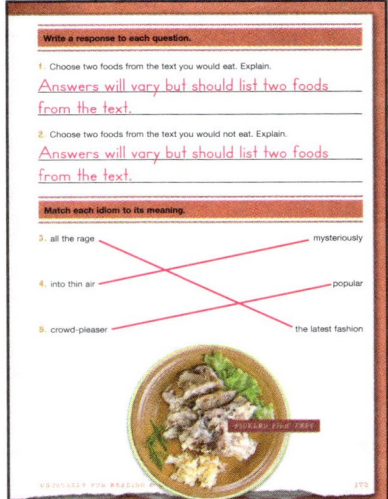

Page 173

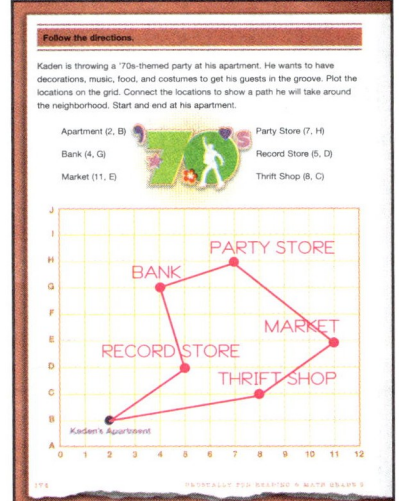

Page 174

# Answer Key

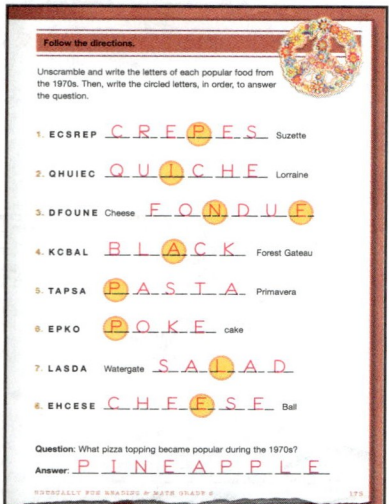

Page 175

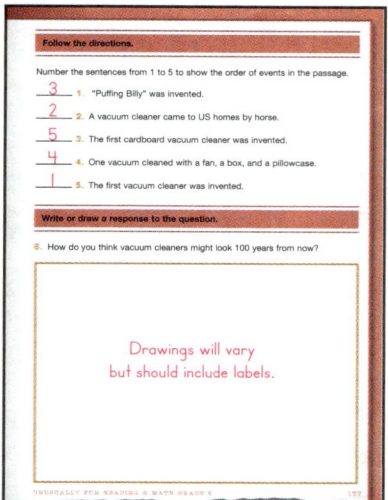

Page 177

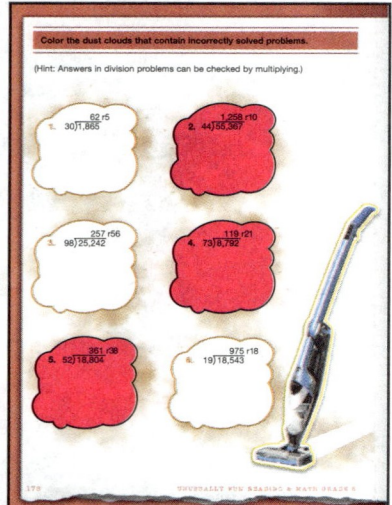

Page 178

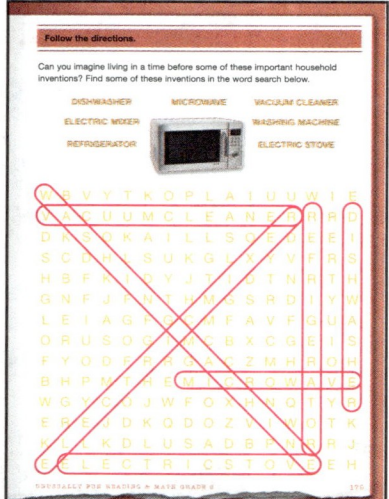

Page 179

# Answer Key

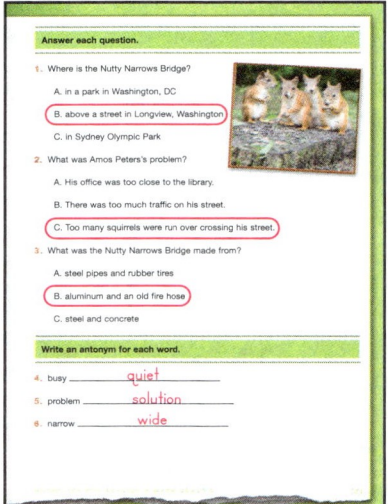

Page 181

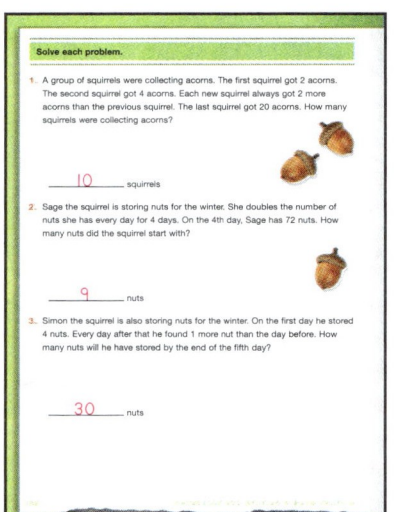

Page 182

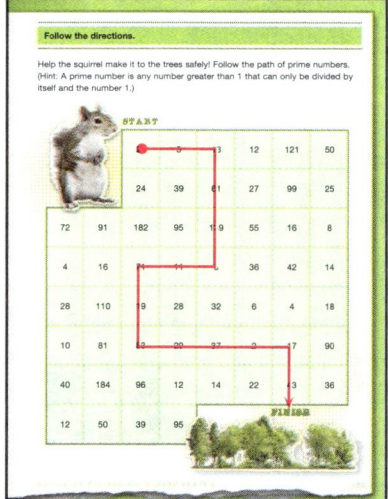

Page 183

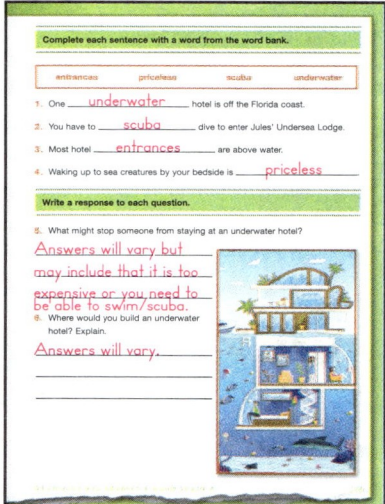

Page 185

# Answer Key

### Page 186

**Solve each problem.**
(Hint: To find volume, use the formula V = l × w × h.)

1. Finn is staying in an underwater hotel room. His room is 14 feet long, 16 feet wide, and 9 feet tall. What is the volume of Finn's room?

   **2,016** cubic feet

2. Isla is also staying in an underwater hotel room. Her room is 6 yards long, 5 yards wide, and 4 yards high. What is the volume of Isla's room?

   **120** cubic yards

3. The underwater hotel has a restaurant. The restaurant is 15 meters long, 17 meters wide, and 5 meters high. What is the volume of the restaurant?

   **1,275** cubic meters

### Page 187

**Follow the directions.**

Use the information from the passage and the clues below to figure out in which hotel each guest stayed.

1. Eli relaxes in his underwater hotel room and stares out the floor to ceiling windows. He sees an octopus swim by!
   Where is Eli staying? **Tanzania**

2. Mila is staying at an underwater lodge. She booked an underwater tour during her stay. She has to scuba dive to get to the lobby!
   Where is Mila staying? **Florida**

3. Wyatt is excited for his underwater hotel visit. He eats at the underwater restaurant and watches the sea creatures swim by. He sees a black-tipped reef shark and a sting ray.
   Where is Wyatt staying? **China**

4. River saved up $500 so she could stay in an underwater hotel room. She is planning to stay for two nights.
   Where is River staying? **Sweden**

### Page 189

**Complete each sentence with a word from the text.**

1. Monkey Island was first called **Morgan Island**
2. At least **4,000** monkeys run around Monkey Island.
3. Scientists have used the monkeys for **medical** testing.

**Write the transition words and events from the last paragraph.**

4. **First,**
   **the monkeys need their space.**
5. **Also,**
   **humans carry germs and diseases.**
6. **Last,**
   **monkeys are wild animals.**

### Page 190

**Solve each problem.**

1. If there are 4,000 monkeys on Monkey Island and 3/4 are female, how many male monkeys are on the island?

   **1,000** male monkeys

2. If 1/4 of the female monkeys have 2 babies each, how many babies would there be?

   **1,500** babies

3. There are 4,000 monkeys. Of the total number of monkeys, 3/8 of the monkeys' favorite food is seeds and 3/16 of the monkeys' favorite food is insects. How many of the monkeys have a favorite food that isn't seeds or insects? Find the answer in number of monkeys and as a fraction.

   **1,750** monkeys
   **7/16** monkeys

# Answer Key

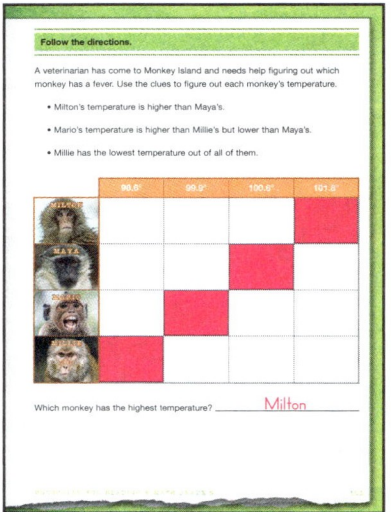

Page 191

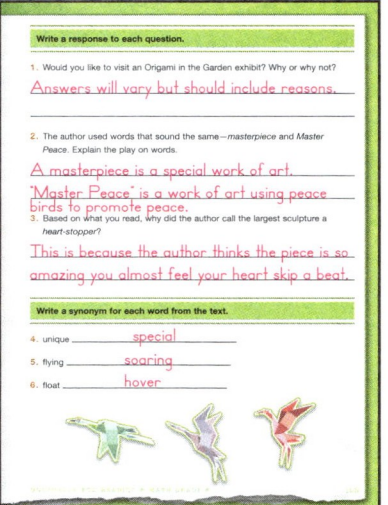

Page 193

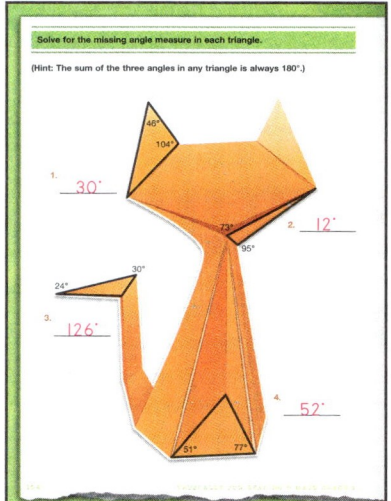

Page 194

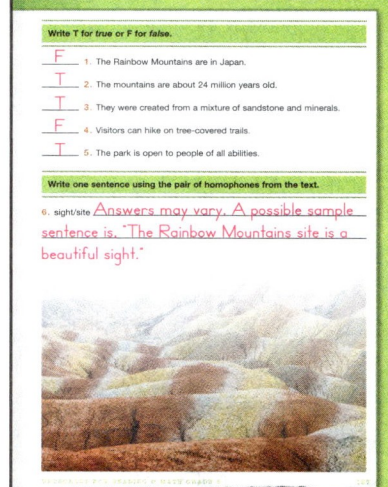

Page 197

# Answer Key

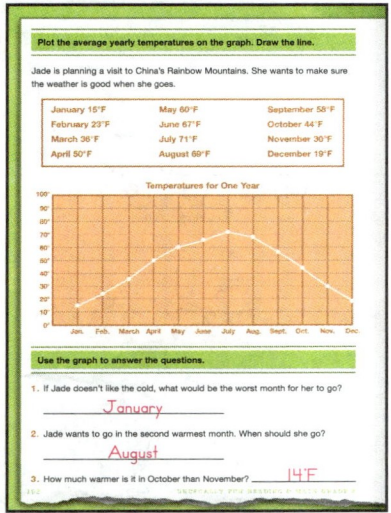

Page 198     Page 199

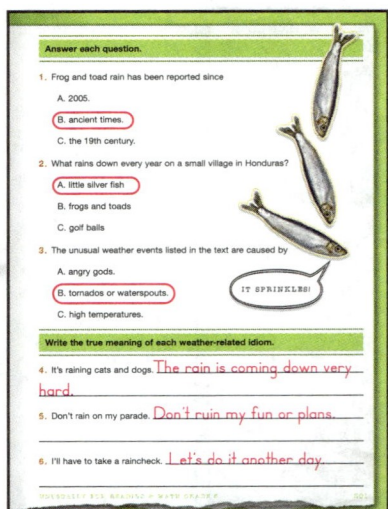 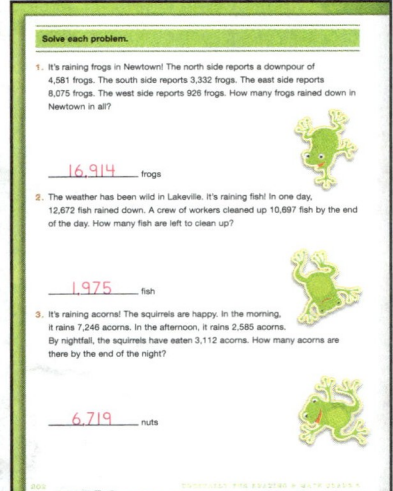 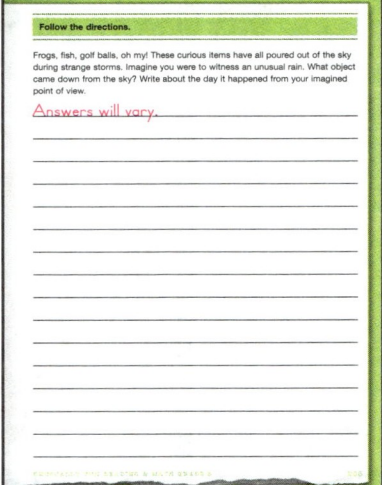

Page 201     Page 202     Page 203

# Answer Key

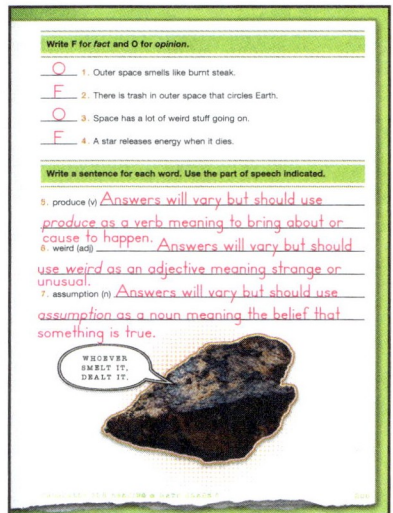

Page 205

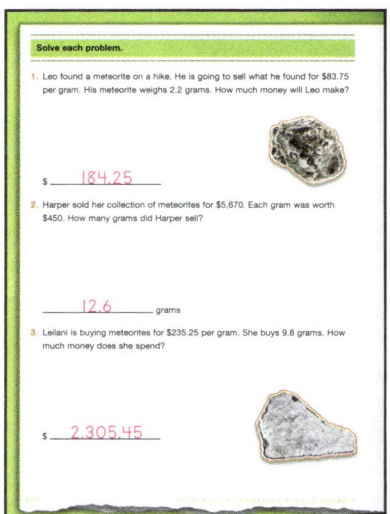

Page 206

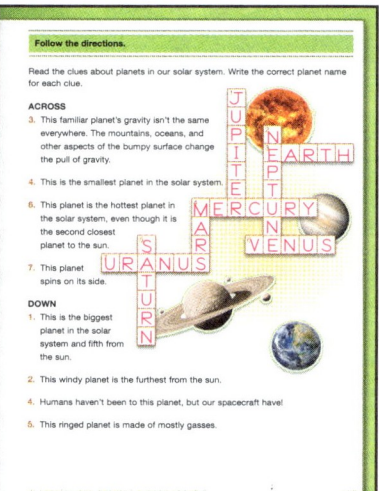

Page 207

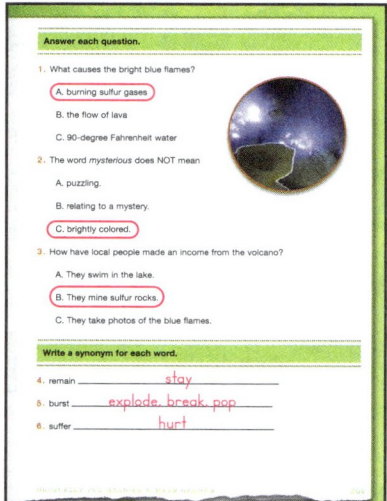

Page 209

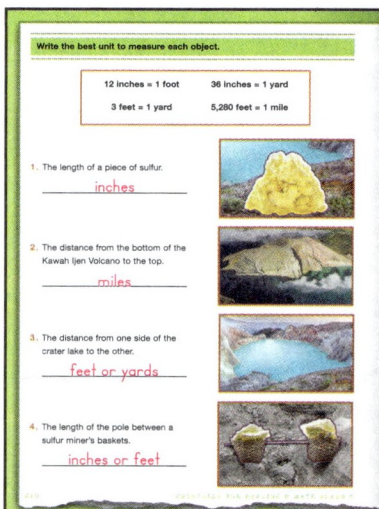

Page 210

# Answer Key

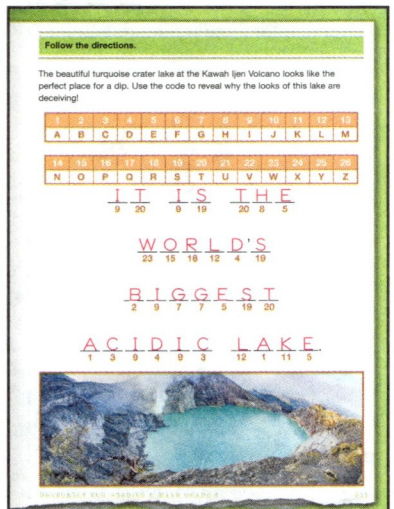
Page 211

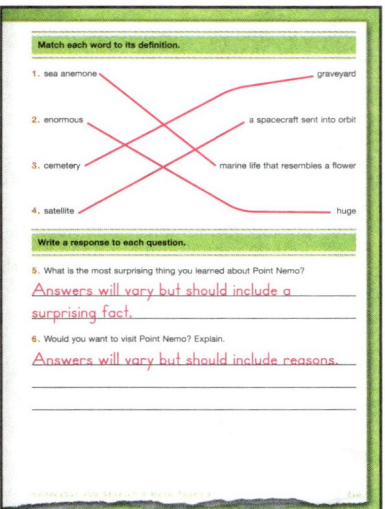
Page 213

Page 214

Page 215

PHOTO/ART CREDITS: Cover ©PrasongTakham/Shutterstock.com, ©autsawin uttisin/Shutterstock.com, ©phototrip/Getty Images, ©malerapaso/Getty Images, ©Aleksei Potov/Shutterstock.com, ©Anatoliy Karlyuk/Shutterstock.com, ©YSK1/Shutterstock.com, ©Alla Laurent/Shutterstock.com, ©Markohanzekovic/Shutterstock.com; p4 ©Agnieszka Bacal/Shutterstock.com, ©Joshua Janes; p5 ©Tasha Drik/Shutterstock.com, ©Liliya Butenko/Shutterstock.com; p6 ©N.Savranska/Shutterstock.com; p7 ©Joshua Janes; p8 ©Joshua Janes, ©Imagine China/Newscom, ©REUTERS/Alamy Stock Photo/©RUSSELL CHEYNE; p9 ©Hung Chung Chih/Shutterstock.com; p10 ©AlsuSh/Shutterstock.com; p11 ©Eakdesign/Shutterstock.com, ©mrjohnblack/Shutterstock.com; p12 ©Zaur Rahimov/Shutterstock.com, ©Ethan Daniels/Shutterstock.com, ©Shpatak/Shutterstock.com; p13 ©Joshua Janes; p14 ©Alexander_P/Shutterstock.com; p15 ©Yevheniia Rodina/Shutterstock.com, ©Shpatak/Shutterstock.com; p16 Nature Picture Library/Alamy Stock Photo/©Sandesh Kadur; p17 ©Smokeyjo/Getty Images, ©Svetsol/Shutterstock.com; p19 ©GoodStudio/Shutterstock.com, ©xpixel/Shutterstock.com; p20 ©krusto/Shutterstock.com, ©Ilya unknown/Shutterstock.com, ©Stefan Ziemendorff/Shutterstock.com; p21 ©imageBROKER/Fabio Pupin/Newscom; p22 ©jhonatan bahtiar/Shutterstock.com; p23 ©alex7370/Shutterstock.com; p24 ©phototrip/Getty Images, ©Pictogram studio/Shutterstock.com, ©soo hee kim/Shutterstock; p25 ©Martin Pelanek/Shutterstock.com; p26 ©Scrudje/Shutterstock.com, ©Joshua Janes; p28 ©Line and Circle/Shutterstock.com, ©Claireb1297/Shutterstock.com; p29 ©Memo Angeles/Shutterstock.com, ©Vladimir Konstantinov/Shutterstock.com, ©nikiteev_konstantin/Shutterstock.com; p31 ©gg-foto/Shutterstock.com; p32 ©Amitrane/Shutterstock.com, ©ayax/Shutterstock.com; p33 ©Daniel J. Rao/Shutterstock.com, Gui Jorge/Shutterstock.com; p34 ©vatrushka67/Getty Images; p35 ©CHANYA_B/Shutterstock.com; p36 ©Katrina Lee/Shutterstock.com, ©Biggy TLC/Shutterstock.com, ©Chinnapong/Shutterstock.com; p38 ©jgareri/Getty Images; p39 ©Teguh Mujiono/Shutterstock.com, ©Lynne Schwaner; p40 ©Janis Abolins/Shutterstock.com, ©Aruna Kalutanthri/Shutterstock.com; p41 ©Merrimon Crawford/Shutterstock.com; p42 ©Phatthanun Kaewsuwan/Shutterstock.com; p43 ©Annmarie Young/Shutterstock.com; p44 ©Rvector/Shutterstock.com, ©Emre Dikici/Shutterstock.com; p45 ©PetlinDmitry/Shutterstock.com; p47 ©Brian Lasenby/Shutterstock.com, ©Arno Dietz/Shutterstock.com, ©Keneva Photography/Shutterstock.com, ©Touched by light images/Shutterstock.com; p48 ©Andrey_Kuzmin/Shutterstock.com; p49 ©Iryna Kuznetsova/Shutterstock.com; p50 ©Valeriia Soloveva/Shutterstock.com; p51 ©cammep/Shutterstock.com, ©Elizabeth Foley/Shutterstock.com; p52 ©FixiPixi_Design_Studio/Shutterstock.com, ©Dennis van de Water/Shutterstock.com, ©Lightboxx/Shutterstock.com, ©AnnstasAg/Shutterstock.com, ©GoodStudio/Shutterstock.com; p54 ©Dennis van de Water/Shutterstock.com, ©Paul Reeves Photography/Shutterstock.com, ©Lightboxx/Shutterstock.com, ©Matthias Kern Wildlife/Shutterstock.com, ©Roberto Dantoni/Shutterstock.com; p56 ©Paul Marcus/Shutterstock.com, ©Alvaro Cabrera Jimenez/Shutterstock.com; p57 ©somdul/Shutterstock.com; p59 ©adipra52/Shutterstock.com; p60 ©Anton Prohorov/Shutterstock.com, ©Stefan Lambauer/Shutterstock.com; p61 ©Cast Of Thousands/Shutterstock.com; p62 ©Lynne Schwaner; p63 ©Tymonko Galyna/Shutterstock.com; p64 ©Heiko Kiera/Shutterstock.com, ©ShutterOK/Shutterstock.com, ©Bahruz Rzayev/Shutterstock.com, ©Matveev Aleksandr/Shutterstock.com, ©Willie Pena/Shutterstock.com; p65 ©Victoria Ditkovsky/Shutterstock.com; p66 ©ClassicVector/Shutterstock.com; p67 ©Sararoom Design/Shutterstock.com, ©Macrovector/Shutterstock.com; p68 ©Mr.Creative/Shutterstock.com, ©IMG Stock Studio/Shutterstock.com, ©New Africa/Shutterstock.com, ©Max4e Photo/Shutterstock.com; p69 ©WILLSIE/Getty Images; p70 ©New Africa/Shutterstock.com, ©Joshua Janes; p71 ©Sharomka/Shutterstock.com; p72 ©Barudak.lier/Shutterstock.com, ©ThamKC/Shutterstock.com, ©airdone/Shutterstock.com; p74 ©phive/Shutterstock.com; p76 ©Kilroy79/Shutterstock.com, ©PicturePartners/Getty Images, ©Hamik/Shutterstock.com, ©Cornelia Scheidt/Shutterstock.com; p77 ©Kate Garyuk/Shutterstock.com; p78 ©Kuznetsov Dmitriy/Shutterstock.com; p79 ©Slanapotam/Shutterstock.com; p80 ©serazetdinov/Shutterstock.com, ©Maks Narodenko/Shutterstock.com, ©Abaca Press/Europa Press/Abaca/Sipa USA/Newscom; p81 ©Alessandro Vargiu/ZUMAPRESS/Newscom, ©Maks Narodenko/Shutterstock.com; p82 ©Jirik V/Shutterstock.com, ©photka/Shutterstock.com; p83 ©donatas1205/Shutterstock.com; p84 ©M-vector/Shutterstock.com, ©Africa Studio/Shutterstock.com, ©Nerthuz/Shutterstock.com, ©Joshua Janes; p86 ©Mau Horng/Shutterstock.com, ©fieldwork/Shutterstock.com, ©pics five/Shutterstock.com, ©Charlotte Lake/Shutterstock.com; ©New Africa/Shutterstock.com, ©Wongsakorn Dulyavit/Shutterstock.com; p87 ©Triff/Shutterstock.com, ©GalapagosPhoto/Shutterstock.com, ©Charlotte Lake/Shutterstock.com; p88 ©digidreamgrafix/Shutterstock.com, ©RedKoala/Shutterstock.com; p90 ©Madlen/Shutterstock.com; p91 ©Rawpixel/Shutterstock.com, ©TWINS DESIGN STUDIO/Shutterstock.com; p92 ©Manglayang Studio/Shutterstock.com, ©Susan Law Cain/Shutterstock.com, ©Studio DMM Photography, ©Designs & Art/Shutterstock.com, ©Vera_Chan/Shutterstock.com; p93 ©wet nose/Shutterstock.com; p95 ©photolinc/Shutterstock.com, ©demidoff/Shutterstock.com, ©kustomer/Shutterstock.com, ©Rawpixel.com/Shutterstock.com; p96 ©LWY Partnership/Shutterstock.com, ©sruilk/Shutterstock.com, ©MATHILDE.LR/Shutterstock.com; p97 ©Naddya/Shutterstock.com; p98 ©bane.m/Shutterstock.com, ©Victor Brave/Shutterstock.com; p99 ©5 second Studio/Shutterstock.com; p100 ©Svetlana Zharskaya/Shutterstock.com, ©nattanan726/Shutterstock.com, ©SherSS/Shutterstock.com, ©Novikov Alex/Shutterstock.com; p101 ©angelo gilardelli/Shutterstock.com; p101 ©Dionisvera/Shutterstock.com; p102 ©Marti Bug Catcher/Shutterstock.com; p104 ©bearsky23/Shutterstock.com, ©kei907/Shutterstock.com; p105 ©Just dance/Shutterstock.com; p106 ©gresei/Shutterstock.com; p107 ©3445128471/Shutterstock.com, ©BUTENKOV ALEKSEI/Shutterstock.com; p108 ©HN Works/Shutterstock.com, ©James Woodson/Getty Images; p109 Dancestrokes/Shutterstock.com; p110 ©TMvectorart/Shutterstock.com; p112 ©johnjohnson/Shutterstock.com, ©KanphotoSS/Shutterstock.com, ©comgi/Shutterstock.com; p113 ©Say_cheese/Getty Images; p114 ©Fotokolia/Shutterstock.com, ©Dmitriev Mikhail/Shutterstock.com; p115 ©Lifestyle Travel Photo/Shutterstock.com, ©Nitr/Shutterstock.com; p116 ©Net Vector/Shutterstock.com, ©Lucy Left/Shutterstock.com; p117 ©Lucy Left/Shutterstock.com; p119 ©Inara Prusakova/Shutterstock.com; p120 ©BlueberryPie/Shutterstock.com, ©logika600/Shutterstock.com; p123 ©Kozlik/Shutterstock.com; p124 ©tmn art/Shutterstock.com, ©Helder Almeida/Shutterstock.com; p125 ©Matej Kastelic/Shutterstock.com; p127 ©LesinkaVector/Shutterstock.com, ©svetalik/Shutterstock.com; p128 ©Nikolai Moiseenko/Shutterstock.com, ©Joshua Janes; p129 ©Krakenimages.com/Shutterstock.com; p130 ©Unicraft/Shutterstock.com; p131 ©Yellow Cat/Shutterstock.com, ©photastic/Shutterstock.com; p132 ©Evgeniy Kalinovskiy/Shutterstock.com, ©BW Folsom/Shutterstock.com, ©grmarc/Shutterstock.com; p134 ©Brand X Pictures/Getty Images; p135 ©Rawpixel.com/Shutterstock.com; p136 ©popicon/Shutterstock.com, ©Nata-Lia/Shutterstock.com, ©3D River/Shutterstock.com; p137 ©cenkerdem/Getty Images; p138 ©ambassador806/Getty Images, ©Rich Carey/Shutterstock.com; p140 ©EmBaSy/Shutterstock.com, ©Murad Aziz/Shutterstock.com; p141 ©HomeArt/Shutterstock.com, ©Murad Aziz/Shutterstock.com; p144 ©KASUE/Shutterstock.com, ©slobo/Getty Images; p145 ©grey_and/Shutterstock.com; p146 ©grey_and/Shutterstock.com; p148 ©Chann Stock/Shutterstock.com, ©Noel V. Baebler/Shutterstock.com, ©Ministr-84/Shutterstock.com, ©ADragan/Shutterstock.com; p149 ©Alexander Lukatskiy/Shutterstock.com; p150 ©Guzel Studio/Shutterstock.com, ©Fotofermer/Shutterstock.com; p151 ©amenic181/Shutterstock.com, ©PavelNemzorov/Shutterstock.com, ©Joe Gough/Shutterstock.com; p152 ©kzww/Shutterstock.com, ©Protasov AN/Shutterstock.com, ©AlenKadr/Shutterstock.com, ©big Stocker/Shutterstock.com.

p153 ©Liudmila Klymenko/Shutterstock.com; p154 ©Romariolen/Shutterstock.com; p155 ©Protasov AN/Shutterstock.com, ©subarashii21/Getty Images, ©Iryna/Getty Images; p156 ©PhotoStockImage/Shutterstock.com, ©George Dolgikh/Shutterstock.com, ©Tukunen/Shutterstock.com; p157 ©OlgaMiltsova/Getty Images; p158 ©Lightspring/Shutterstock.com; p159 ©amenic181/Shutterstock.com, ©Valentina Razumova/Shutterstock.com, ©Danny Smythe/Shutterstock.com; p160 ©Krakenimages.com/Shutterstock.com; p162 ©Sergio33/Shutterstock.com, ©art nick/Shutterstock.com; p164 ©D.Cz./Shutterstock.com, ©HappyPictures/Shutterstock.com, ©Cosmic_Design/Shutterstock.com; p165 ©HappyPictures/Shutterstock.com; p166 ©PCH.Vector/Shutterstock.com; p167 ©dwi putra stock/Shutterstock.com, ©Pixel-Shot/Shutterstock.com, ©Diana_Karch/Shutterstock.com, ©Tim UR/Shutterstock.com; p168 ©Northwestern University, ©denvitruk/Shutterstock.com, ©higyou/Getty Images; p169 ©Arianayah/Shutterstock.com; p170 ©Oleksii Arseniuk/Shutterstock.com; p171 ©Media Whale Stock/Shutterstock.com; p172 ©bsd studio/Shutterstock.com, ©Lonely Walker/Shutterstock.com, ©Michael Kraus/Shutterstock.com; p173 ©Fanfo/Shutterstock.com; p174 ©MisterStock/Shutterstock.com; p175 ©EVA105/Shutterstock.com; p176 ©anjoirina/Shutterstock.com, ©Minh Do/Shutterstock.com, ©Adil Abdrakhmanov/Getty Images; p178 ©Tatiana Popova/Shutterstock.com, ©32 pixels/Shutterstock.com; p179 ©Hurst Photo/Shutterstock.com; p180 ©IrinaK/Shutterstock.com, ©DrimaFilm/Shutterstock.com, ©Irvan Pratama/Shutterstock.com; p181 ©Tntk/Shutterstock.com; p182 ©Dionisvera/Shutterstock.com; p183 ©IrinaK/Shutterstock.com, ©Artiste2d3d/Shutterstock.com; p184 ©Mekan Photography/Shutterstock.com, ©XiXinXing/Getty Images, ©Mega Pixel/Shutterstock.com, ©Nadiinko/Shutterstock.com; p185 ©Seahorse Vector/Shutterstock.com; p186 ©Mikumi/Getty Images; p187 ©Andrei Armiagov/Shutterstock.com; p188 ©Vaclav Krivsky/Shutterstock.com, ©Maksym Gorpenyuk/Shutterstock.com; p189 ©Sanchos303/Shutterstock.com; p190 ©apple2499/Shutterstock.com; p191 ©Sutiwat Vejsuparkul/Shutterstock.com, ©PetrP/Shutterstock.com, ©apiguide/Shutterstock.com, ©Musafar Ali KP/Shutterstock.com; p192 ©AG/Getty Images, ©icondesigner/Shutterstock.com; p193 ©seamartini/Getty Images; p194 ©Vectors Bang/Shutterstock.com; p195 ©Julia Savko/Getty Images; p196 ©J-Chan studio/Shutterstock.com, ©pne/Shutterstock.com; p197 ©Ana Flasker/Shutterstock.com; p199 ©SCStock/Getty Images; p200 ©Joshua Janes, ©BBA Photography/Shutterstock.com; p201 ©Graeme Dawes/Shutterstock.com; p202 ©Net Vector/Shutterstock.com; p204 ©Dima Zel/Shutterstock.com, ©davooda/Shutterstock.com; p205 ©Misha Beliy/Shutterstock.com; p206 ©Bjoern Wylezich/Shutterstock.com, ©Pavel Gabzdyl/Shutterstock.com; p207 ©19 STUDIO/Shutterstock.com; p208 ©Ayub Irawan/Shutterstock.com, ©thanmano/Shutterstock.com; p209 ©Assawin/Getty Images; p210 ©Sebastian Janicki/Shutterstock.com, ©Putu Artana/Shutterstock.com, ©Mazur Travel/Shutterstock.com, ©Larcsky789/Shutterstock.com; p211 ©DPST/Newscom; p212 ©Oliver Denker/Shutterstock.com, ©omibomotu/shutterstock.com; p214 ©irin-k/Shutterstock.com, ©Sergiy1975/Shutterstock.com, ©Maria Spb/Shutterstock.com, ©Karel Kralovec/Shutterstock.com; p215 ©Yurij Omelchenko/Shutterstock.com, ©Mr Dasenna/Shutterstock.com, ©Diana_Karch/Shutterstock.com; all interior background pages ©PrasongTakham/Shutterstock.com